DRUG ABUSE

A-Z

Gilda and Melvin Berger

— A-Z Reference Series —

ENSLOW PUBLISHERS, INC.
Bloy St. & Ramsey Ave.   P.O. Box 38
Box 777   Aldershot
Hillside, N.J. 07205   Hants GU12 6BP
U.S.A.   U.K.

Library of Congress Cataloging-in-Publication Data

Berger, Gilda.
    Drug Abuse A-Z / by Gilda and Melvin Berger.

    p. cm. — (A-Z reference series)

    Bibliography: p.

    ISBN 0-89490-193-1

    1. Drug abuse—Dictionaries, Juvenile. 2. Drugs—Dictionaries, Juvenile.
I. Berger, Melvin. II. Title. III. Title: Drug abuse A-Z. IV. Series.

RC564.B473 1990
362.29'03—dc20   89-1512
                             CIP
                             AC

Printed in the United States of America

10 9 8 7 6 5 4 3 2 1

CONTENTS

INTRODUCTION

Drug Abuse A–Z is a dictionary-like guide to the entire world of drug abuse—the scientific names, trade names, and slang names of the drugs; how, when, and why the drugs are taken; the effects of the drugs in ordinary doses and overdoses; the special equipment of drug users; and the special vocabulary of the drug culture.

Strictly speaking, *any* drug taken for nonmedical or recreational purpose, to affect a person's mind or body in ways the user considers pleasant and enjoyable, may form a pattern of abuse. In this book, the term drug abuse refers specifically to any drug-induced behaviors that seriously affect the user's health, ability to earn a living, or social well-being.

Drug abuse is a widespread problem that makes individual drug users the prime victims. But drugs also affect all of us, wherever we live and whatever we do. Drug abuse can cause serious physical and mental deterioration. The problem can tear apart the family structure and make learning difficult. Difficulties on the job due to drug abuse make it hard for employers to run their businesses. Stealing from employers or from individuals to get money for drugs causes pain and economic loss to the victims. Arrests and jailings of drug users and dealers puts a strain on law enforcement officials and the criminal justice system; the cost to taxpayers is enormous. The millions of dollars spent on illegal drugs in America encourages criminal activity and robs the government of tax revenues.

For all these reasons—and many more—the subject of drug abuse is extremely important. As a way of considering this vast subject, experts have classified the drugs according to their primary effects on the body. Thus, the eight basic drug classifications are as follows: antidepressants, antianxiety tranquilizers, antipsychotic tranquilizers, cannabis, hallucinogens, narcotics, sedative/hypnotics, and stimulants. More information on each classification and its examples can be found in the main entry section.

Antidepressant drugs are substances that improve a person's mood and are commonly used in the treatment of depression. Depression is a psychiatric problem that is characterized by a loss of interest in most aspects of life, a slowing-down of activity, a feeling of worthlessness, and sometimes suicidal thoughts. When used for nonmedical purposes, antidepressant drugs have little impact on mood and do not give immediate sensations of pleasure. Nevertheless, they have been found to increase the effect of other drugs that depress the central nervous system, including alcohol, antihistamines, barbiturates, narcotics, sedatives, and tranquilizers. Two of the main types of antidepressants are ELAVIL and TOFRANIL.

Antianxiety tranquilizers are drugs that have a calming effect on the central nervous system, relieve anxiety and tension, and sometimes relax the skeletal muscles. The drugs have been shown to have undesirable side effects and to be habit-forming. Tranquilizers are especially dangerous as they intensify the effects of other depressants such as the opiates, barbiturates, and alcohol. When taken together with any of the other depressants, tranquilizers can cause coma and even death. LIBRIUM and VALIUM are two examples of antianxiety tranquilizers that produce effects like alcohol and barbiturates, and they are often abused.

Antipsychotic tranquilizers is a major classification of drugs commonly used to treat serious psychiatric problems. The drugs, such as THORAZINE, are rarely used nonmedically, because they do not produce euphoric effects and generally give unpleasant side effects. Still, the drugs are sometimes preferred to barbiturates as calming agents because they do not cause physical dependence and even in large doses do not result in coma.

Cannabis is a general term used to refer to various preparations, such as HASHISH, HASH OIL, and MARIJUANA, that are consumed for their intoxicating effects. The intensity of the reactions depend on such factors as the potency of the drug, the mood and expectations of the user, and the environment in which the drug is taken. Cannabis is classified in a category of its own, though its effects are similar to those of the depressants, stimulants, and hallucinogens.

Hallucinogens are a group of natural and man-made drugs whose primary effect is to distort the senses. The chief result is hallucinations—experiences that have nothing to do with reality. Included in this classification are LSD, MDA, and PCP. Although other drugs, such as alcohol or cannabis, may produce hallucinations, they are not considered hallucinogens because this is not the usual effect that is expected or experienced.

Narcotics generally refers to any substance that dulls a person's senses. Drugs in this class are capable of narcosis—of producing a sense of well-being in small doses and lethargy, drowsiness, or coma when taken in large amounts. This classification includes OPIUM, MORPHINE, and HEROIN. Since the early 20th century, the term came to mean any disapproved, illicit drug, or a drug that produced sleep or hallucination and appeared addicting or harmful.

Sedative/Hypnotics are a class of drugs that causes relaxation, calmness, and sedation in low doses and sleep in higher doses. The class includes ALCOHOL, such as distilled liquors and wine, BARBITURATES, such as PENTOTHAL SODIUM, nonbarbiturates, such as METHAQUALONE (QUAALUDE), and STIMULANTS, such as BENZEDRINE and RITALIN.

Before presenting the main body of drug abuse terms, *Drug Abuse A–Z* offers you, the reader, some brief descriptions of the most significant federal legislation that is related to drug abuse. The purpose is to provide a historical perspective for the present classifications of "controlled substances," or drugs that are subject to abuse.

If you wish the addresses or telephone numbers of government agencies and private organizations that can provide more information on drug abuse or on specific drugs, please turn to the **For Further Information** section in the back of the book.

For a listing of the major sources of information for *Drug Abuse A–Z*, please see **References,** also listed after the main entries. Keep in mind, though, that these sources were supplemented with considerable material from current newspapers and magazines.

MAJOR FEDERAL DRUG LAWS

Drug abuse is a problem that societies experience in historical cycles. Around the turn of the century, the United States suffered from an epidemic of drug use that rivals that of today. Doctors freely dispensed such dependence-producing drugs as cocaine, morphine, and heroin to patients eager to get instant relief from pain. A wide assortment of varied drugs, readily available from a totally unregulated patent medicine industry, were enthusiastically foisted on the American public by everyone from skillful doctors to fraudulent hucksters.

The Harrison Act of 1914 was the first federal narcotics law that attempted to make the use of certain drugs an illegal activity. The law had three main provisions:

1. Anyone producing or distributing narcotics had to register with the federal government and keep records of all transactions.

2. Anyone buying or selling a narcotic had to pay a tax of one cent per ounce.

3. Narcotics could only be bought with a prescription.

The purpose of the bill was to allow the government to keep track of drug transactions and of those involved in the drug trade. It did, however, include penalties for anyone found with untaxed or unrecorded drugs. The Treasury Department was made responsible for enforcing the act.

Requiring addicts and distributors of narcotics to register with the Treasury Department made drug use a punishable violation, even if prescribed by a doctor. Physicians became unwilling to dispense dependence-producing drugs under any circumstance. The result was that drug use actually increased. People who had been on drugs needed a source for drugs, and an illegal marketplace filled that need.

By the early 1920s, the use of heroin, in particular, was of epidemic proportions. The increase in drug traffickers peddling their wares to increasing numbers of users led to a call for more legislation. The passage of the Narcotic Drugs Import and Export Act of 1922 empowered the Federal Narcotics Control Board to determine how much opium, cocaine, and their derivatives needed to be imported to this country to fulfill legitimate medical needs. Further, anyone found in possession of a drug without a prescription was assumed to have obtained the drug illegally, which was a federal crime. (This act was replaced by the Controlled Substances Act of 1970.)

In the 1930s, a barrage of medical, law enforcement, and legislative efforts slowed the tide of narcotic addiction for a while at least. But it was about this time that marijuana began flooding the market. Within a few years, marijuana was placed in the same illegal category as opium and cocaine.

In 1932, the National Conference of Commissioners on Uniform State Laws, a private semi-official organization, proposed a uniform drug law for enactment by the individual states. Passed into law by most states between 1933 and 1937, the major provisions of the Uniform State Narcotic Drug Act were to classify marijuana as an opiate and cocaine as a narcotic and to make it a criminal offense to possess marijuana.

The Marijuana Tax Act of 1937 was a federal act that had several purposes: To raise revenues, to identify all persons involved with marijuana, and to discourage recreational, nonmedical use of the drug. The main provisions of the act were:

1. All persons using marijuana for legitimate medical purposes must pay a tax of $1.00 per ounce.

2. All persons using it for nonmedical purposes must pay a tax of $100.00 per ounce.

3. All persons who do not comply with the act's provisions are subject to penalties for tax evasion.

The next decade, the 1940s, began with the virtual disappearance of large-scale drug-taking. The success was believed due, not to the enactment of laws and the opening of treatment facilities, but to the interruption in supply routes of drugs from Asia and Europe as a result of World War II. With the end of the war, the opium-heroin trafficking networks were reestablished, and shipments of illegal narcotics began to reach America.

The large number of social problems in the 1950s led to the Narcotic Drug Control Act of 1956. This act outlawed heroin and increased the penalties for transporting, smuggling, or selling heroin or marijuana. At the same time, it lowered the restrictions on surveillance of known drug traffickers and made it easier to obtain search warrants in narcotics cases. Federal narcotics agents were also empowered to make arrests without warrants for any drug violations they observed. (Most of the provisions of this act were repealed by the Drug Abuse Act of 1970.)

During the revolutionary 1960s, drugs moved from the more marginal points of society—the inner-city ghettos and underground artists' culture—to the very mainstream of American life. Middle-class and young adult populations of both rural and urban America became caught up in drug use and abuse. One significant piece of legislation from this time is the Drug Abuse Control Amendment of 1965.

Also known as the Harris-Dodd Act, it was an amendment to food, drug, and cosmetic legislation that classified certain drugs, including particular amphetamines, barbiturates, hallucinogens, tranquilizers, and nonbarbiturate sedative/hypnotics, as "dangerous drugs" and placed these drugs under tight federal control. The act requires that no person possess any of these drugs except for personal or family use and that only authorized manufacturers and suppliers may sell the drugs. Furthermore, full records must be kept of all manufacture and sales; prescriptions are limited to five refills within a six-month period.

The Narcotic Addict Rehabilitation Act of 1966 is a law that establishes the principle of civil commitment of drug abusers to in-hospital treatment, followed by a period of out-patient support and supervision within their own communities. The persons eligible for this program are narcotic addicts charged with certain crimes who ask to be committed for treatment, addicts convicted of crimes who are ordered into treatment by the court, and addicts who voluntarily ask to be committed.

By the end of the 1960s, drug-taking had become part and parcel of American social life. Using drugs as a form of relaxation and to form friendships and find love became a fairly commonplace thing to do.

In addition to heroin, there were now the strong stimulants and the amphetamines. As legislators attempted to stamp out amphetamine use, young users simply turned to such easily obtainable drugs as Quaaludes. Thus, one drug problem was replaced by another, and the drug epidemic continued.

During the 1970s, marijuana use grew until it reached as many as an estimated 50 million Americans in every walk of life and every level of society. An important piece of legislation that attempted to respond to this widespread problem is the Controlled Substances

Act of 1970. This act establishes five "schedules," or classifications, of "controlled substances," or drugs that are subject to abuse.

Schedule I. This group includes heroin, marijuana, LSD, mescaline, psilocybin, and other drugs that are thought to have a high potential for abuse and have no known medical use in the United States. Schedule I drugs can only be obtained legally for limited research purposes.

Schedule II. Morphine, methadone, Demerol, methaqualone, and certain short-acting barbiturates and amphetamines are substances that differ from the Schedule I drugs in that they have some currently accepted medical uses. The manufacture and sale of these drugs are carefully controlled, and they may be obtained only with a doctor's nonrefillable prescription.

Schedule III. Doriden, paregoric, barbiturates, and other drugs with some abuse potential make up this category. Fewer controls exist for these substances than for Schedule II drugs. For example, no prescription refills may be given after six months.

Schedule IV. Substances, such as Phenobarbital, Placidyl, chloralhydrate, meprobamate, and certain other long-acting barbiturates and antianxiety tranquilizers are considered here. These drugs have less abuse potential than the drugs of Schedule III.

Schedule V. Cough medicines with codeine, which may be sold over the counter in drugstores only to persons over eighteen, with a record kept of the buyer's name are in this group.

Moreover, there was the Drug Abuse Act of 1970, whose full title is the Comprehensive Drug Abuse Prevention and Control Act of 1970. This act, the first major federal drug bill since the Harrison Narcotics Act of 1914, established strict import and export limitations, extended the penalties for trafficking, and set up controls on drugs that had not been regulated before. It did, however, reduce the penalties for possession of an illicit drug.

The 1980s brought certain changes in drug abuse that are being watched very carefully. On the plus side, marijuana and other drug use actually began to decline, especially among high school students. But now a new and perhaps even more serious problem arose. Cocaine began to emerge as the new drug of choice. The extremely dangerous cocaine derivative, crack, disrupted many millions of lives. Huge amounts of money to be made attracted additional traffickers and dealers. An increased supply hooked even more people into heavy drug use. The abuse of methamphetamines, or speed, and the drug called Ecstasy spread among teens and the way they take the drugs.

Experts in many fields question the effectiveness of measures that have been taken to deal with the varied and very serious problems spawned by drug abuse. Lawyers have been joined by doctors, sociologists, psychologists, and others in attempting to cope with the situation. A wide range of drug terms from slang to advanced biomedical terminology has emerged. Many terms change their meanings over time. Other terms may be concise but are often confusing. However, it is important, as we struggle to deal with the alarm many of us feel at what drugs are doing to our society, that we get familiar with the assortment of terms found in the drug abuse field so that we may better talk with and understand one another.

DRUG ABUSE
TERMS
A

A. See **AMPHETAMINES**; see also **LSD**.

AA. Alcoholics Anonymous, a group that helps alcoholics help themselves and each other to become sober and stay sober. At AA meetings, the members share their experiences concerning alcohol. Alcoholics tell how they are able to control their dependency on alcohol. They encourage, advise, and suggest ways to break the drinking habit and to get along without drinking. An informal buddy system is in place to support members when they are under stress and tempted to have a drink. Basically, AA believes that there is no cure for alcoholism. As they put it, "Once an alcoholic, always an alcoholic." But they do hold that alcoholism can be controlled by completely avoiding alcohol.

ABE. A drug that costs five dollars. The name comes from the picture of Abraham Lincoln on the five-dollar bill.

A-BOMB. A cigarette containing a mixture of drugs. The most popular combination is marijuana and heroin.

ABSOLUTE ALCOHOL. Pure alcohol, containing no water or other substances.

ABSORPTION. The passage of a substance, like a drug, across a bodily membrane, such as the lining of the intestines or the skin, and into the bloodstream.

ABSTINENCE. The complete avoidance of some substance or behavior. When someone practices abstinence in regard to drugs, he or she is said to be drug-free.

ABSTINENCE SYNDROME. See **WITHDRAWAL SYNDROME.**

ABUSE, DRUG. See **DRUG ABUSE.**

ACAPULCO GOLD. A type of marijuana grown near the city of Acapulco, Mexico. It is a particularly potent variety and therefore costs an average of about 40 percent more than lower grades. The name comes from its golden-brown color.

ACE. Slang for **MARIJUANA.**

ACETONE. A solvent used in such products as nail polish remover and plastic cements. Used as an inhalant.

ACID. Slang for **LSD.**

ACID DROPPER. Someone who uses LSD.

ACID FREAK. Someone who uses LSD frequently and may appear, dress, and behave in a highly unconventional manner.

ACID HEAD. Someone who is a frequent, heavy user of LSD.

ACID ROCK. A type of rock 'n' roll music made popular in the 1960s that is usually very loud and very repetitive. It is said that the music is inspired by LSD and creates in the listeners the same feelings as an LSD trip. The music started in San Francisco, and the best known acid-rock bands were The Grateful Dead and Jefferson Airplane.

ACID TEST. Sometimes refers to parties held in the 1960s in which LSD was taken. Sometimes refers to a person's ability to take LSD and not suffer any ill effects.

ACTION. The sale or use of drugs.

ACTIVE INGREDIENT. The component in a drug that is most responsible for altering perception or causing harm to users. For example, the active ingredient in opium is morphine, in peyote it is mescaline, and in marijuana it is tetrahydrocannabinol (THC). Also called "active principal."

ACUTE. A condition that is severe, but not of long duration.

ADDICT. Someone with a strong, compulsive need for some substance, often accompanied by physical dependence. The addict depends on the substance to get through each day and to manage his or her affairs. Addicts will often continue using the substance even if it causes illness, means being thrown out of school or losing a job, results in a prison sentence, or breaks up a family.

ADDICTION. The word "addiction" comes from the Latin, *addicere,* which means "to favor" or "to bind" a person to something. Someone with an addiction is so bound to a particular drug or group of drugs that he or she will not, or cannot, stop the drug use.

There is, however, some controversy about the exact definition of addiction. Some say that the term only refers to the compulsive use of a substance resulting in a physical dependency. Others hold that a psychological dependency is also a form of addiction. Generally speaking, though, addiction is the abuse of any substance resulting in either a physical dependency, a psychological dependency, or both. Although addiction usually refers to the use of narcotics and other physical dependence-producing drugs, the term may apply to the abuse of any substance (e.g., alcohol, cigarettes).

Addictive behaviors often result from an experimentation with addictive substances. The pattern of abuse usually starts when people decide they want to enjoy the pleasures these drugs offer. They crave the "high" they can get, the feelings of euphoria, of strength and power, of being able to forget their problems and get rid of their tensions, even though they are aware of the negative, bad side of drug use. They know of the physical and psychological pain that can come as a side effect of drug abuse. Even though many personal, social, and legal difficulties result from a drug habit, some users find the need for pleasure stronger than the fear of pain. They become "hooked"; they develop an addiction. And the concern of the physical discomfort they may suffer if they quit makes the addiction ever stronger.

There are three main ways to treat an addiction:

1. Break the habit by addicting the person to another, less-harmful drug, such as methadone.

2. Use group or individual psychotherapy to eliminate the psychological need for the drug.

3. Make it impossible, usually in either a prison or hospital, for the person to obtain the drug.

ADDICTION-PRONE PERSONALITY. A theory that holds that certain kinds of individuals, with special psychological characteristics, will get involved with drugs and continue to use them in spite of the strong disapproval of society. Some, however, do not accept this position, saying that addicts are not all alike. They come to their addictions for many different reasons and causes.

ADDITIVE EFFECT. The combined action of two drugs when taken together.

ADMINISTRATION. The method by which a drug is introduced into the body. The principal means of administration are by swallowing, inhaling, injecting into a vein, muscle, or under the skin, or by absorption through the surface of the skin, nose, gums, or other mucous membranes (vagina, anus).

ADULTERATION. To change the quality by adding another substance to a drug. The added substance, called an adulterant, could be an inactive material to add bulk or an active material to make the drug more potent.

ADVERSE DRUG REACTION. A negative or unpleasant physical or psychological reaction to a drug. Among the adverse reactions are feelings of losing control, fear of insanity or death, despair and depression, anxiety, tremors, hallucinations, and paranoia. Sometimes called a "bad trip."

AFFECT. A person's emotional feeling and mood.

AFRICAN BLACK. A potent type of hashish, its name coming from its continent of origin and its color.

AFTERCARE. The services provided to an individual after successful completion of a drug treatment program. Designed to help integrate the person in society, aftercare usually includes participation in a self-help group, support in a work program, and follow-up contacts with counselors.

AGITATION. A high level of restlessness and nervousness that is sometimes caused by a drug overdose. It includes tremors, fidgeting, pacing, and hand wringing.

A-HEAD. A frequent, habitual user of amphetamines.

A LA CANONA. Spanish slang expression meaning to suddenly stop the use of heroin. Same as **COLD TURKEY.**

AL-ANON. An organization for helping relatives and friends of alcoholics that is associated with Alcoholics Anonymous.

ALATEEN. An organization for helping the teen-aged children of alcoholic parents that is associated with Alcoholics Anonymous.

ALCOHOL. A chemical compound (C_2H_5OH), also known as ethanol or ethyl alcohol, that is a depressant of the central nervous system. The name is also applied to any beverage, such as beer, wine, or whiskey, that contains alcohol.

Alcohol is the oldest and most widely used social drug. It is made by fermenting grapes or grain to make wine or beer, which then can be distilled to make the more potent distilled drinks, such as whiskey and brandy. The alcohol, which is the intoxicating element in all of these drinks, is found in concentrations of approximately 4 percent in beer, 12 percent in wine, and 50 percent in distilled liquors. A single serving of each of these drinks, therefore, contains about the same amount of alcohol. A 12-ounce can of beer, a 5-ounce glass of wine and a 1 1/2-ounce shot of whiskey all contain approximately a half ounce of alcohol.

When alcohol is swallowed, it passes through the digestive system and is absorbed into the bloodstream, which carries the alcohol to every part of the body, including the brain. Alcohol has its greatest effect in the brain. As a depressant, it lowers the activity of the nerve cells, or neurons. The greater the amount of alcohol, the greater the effect.

The alcohol weakens the part of the brain that controls behavior. At first, this is pleasurable. It releases inhibitions and makes the drinker feel happy and relaxed. But those who go on to have two and a half drinks within an hour find that it also affects their judgment. They may become loud and abusive and find themselves doing things—driving wildly, acting violently, committing crimes—that they would not do when sober.

Five drinks taken in an hour bring the level of alcohol to 0.10 percent. A person tested with a Breathalyzer and found at this concentration of alcohol is considered to be legally drunk. Alcohol in this quantity depresses the parts of the brain responsible for muscle coordination. Speech is slurred. There is a loss of dexterity. Movements are sloppy and not well controlled. Reaction time is slowed down.

With ten drinks within an hour, the blood-alcohol level reaches 0.20 percent. More of the brain is involved, resulting in erratic emotions, with sudden switches from laughter to tears to anger. Judgment, coordination, and perception are all severely affected. The person may pass out and become unconscious.

Twelve drinks in the same period of time can paralyze the person's breathing, leading to either a coma or death.

ALCOHOLIC. Someone suffering from alcoholism.

ALCOHOLISM. The frequent, compulsive consumption of alcohol that causes damage, mental or physical, to the individual or to society. Some divide alcoholism into three levels: Mild—they feel the need for alcohol at social functions; Moderate—they feel the need for alcohol in order to function well, socially and in their occupation, and make a determined effort to obtain the alcohol; Strong—they drink more or less all the time and are willing to go to any lengths to obtain the next drink.

The explanations for alcoholism also fall into three levels: (1) the "need" for the drink in order to feel comfortable, to relax, to relieve boredom, to sleep, to stimulate appetite; (2) the wish to remove inhibitions on subconscious or conscious obsessions, such as anxiety, sexuality, aggressiveness, or inhibited masculinity or feminity; (3) the desire to withdraw from a world that is perceived as dangerous or threatening.

Many people drink, yet not everyone falls prey to alcoholism. And reactions vary considerably, from barely any reaction at all to intoxication with the smallest consumption of alcohol. Some say that alcoholism may be inherited or may be due to a chemical imbalance of the system. Others hold that alcoholism is a disease and beyond the person's control. Still others say it springs from psychological problems.

The evidence for a genetic basis for alcoholism comes from two recent studies that compared the drinking history of sets of identical twins (with the same genes) and fraternal twins (born at the same time, but with different genes). In cases where one identical twin was an alcoholic, the other twin was apt to be one as well. With fraternal twins, however, far fewer pairs of alcoholic twins were found. The other study followed the drinking patterns of children who were adopted before they were six years old. More of the children born to alcoholic parents had drinking problems than did the children of non-drinking parents, no matter the habits of the adoptive parents.

Observations of large populations support the theory that biochemistry plays a role in alcoholism. Asians, for example, have a very low incidence of alcoholism. In the past, this was ascribed to social customs and factors. But recent studies suggest that many Asians actually have unpleasant reactions, including nausea and flushing, to even small amounts of alcohol. A high percentage of Jews also have adverse reactions to alcohol, which may be a partial explanation of the low percentage of Jews who are alcoholics.

One theory, now being tested, is that some people have allergies to alcohol. This then acts as a protection against alcoholism for these individuals.

Another very popular belief is that alcoholism is a disease. Some 80 percent of the American public hold with this position. According to this view, the more a person drinks, the more he or she needs to drink. The disease then progresses from moderate drinking to heavy consumption. And it is a sequence that has little to do with choice or willpower.

A number of researchers in the field insist that alcoholism is basically a psychological problem that springs from mental or emotional causes. As children, they say, the present alcoholics may have been rejected or abused by their parents. Or they were jealous of their mother or father and now drink to bolster their self-image. Maybe they were unsuccessful in school or could not make friends and feel inadequate. Sometimes drinking starts as a rebellion against parents who oppose alcohol. Perhaps it is an effort to cope with homosexual or suicidal tendencies, among many other possible factors.

Government surveys show that alcoholism is widespread. About 9 million men and women, about 6 percent of the population, can be classified as alcoholics. Many millions more are moderate to severe problem drinkers. Nearly all high school seniors, 93 percent, have tried alcohol. Fully 32 percent said that most or all of their friends get drunk at least once a week.

ALICE B. TOKLAS BROWNIES. Brownies or cookies baked with marijuana or hashish. Named after the woman who was the companion of writer Gertrude Stein and who presumably mixed hashish in with a fudge recipe.

ALIENATION. The feeling of being estranged from and dissassociated from others.

ALTERED STATE OF CONSCIOUSNESS. A psychological condition in which an individual's perception of time and place is altered by chemical drugs or by some mental process, such as meditation.

AMANITA MUSCARIA. A poisonous mushroom that produces hallucinations. The common name is fly agaric.

AMINES, SYMPATHOMIMETIC. A group of drugs that prepare the body for a "fight or flight" response. Amphetamines are synthetic sympathomimetic amines.

AMOBARBITAL. A sedative/hypnotic/barbiturate that acts in fifteen to thirty minutes and lasts for three to six hours. The medical dose as a sedative is 20 to 50 milligrams; as a hypnotic (sleeping pill), the dose is 100 to 200 milligrams.

AMPHETAMINES. A general name given to a group of drugs that are similar in some ways to adrenaline and that act as a stimulant on the central nervous system. Scientifically, they are known as sympathomimetic amines. The first amphetamine, 2-phenylisopropylamine, was produced in 1887. Currently there are three types of amphetamines: Amphetamine sulfate (Benzedrine), which is the least potent; Dextroamphetamine sulfate (Dexedrine, Dexamyl), intermediate in potency and with the fewest side effects; Methamphetamine hydrochloride (Methedrine, Desoxyn, Amphedroxyn, Norodin), which is the most potent.

The amphetamines have found several medical uses—as a nasal decongestant, as an energizer, stimulant, and anti-depressant, to treat narcolepsy (involuntary sleep), to control hyperactive children (where the drug has a calming instead of stimulating effect), as a diet aid (since they seem to lessen appetite), and as a general aid to wakefulness, alertness, and feelings of euphoria. Because of their qualities of giving extra energy and keeping the user awake, the Germans, Japanese, Americans, and British all issued amphetamines to their troops during World War II. This contributed to the start of widespread amphetamine abuse. After the war, the surplus pills were sold on the open market.

Physically, the effects of the amphetamines are to constrict the blood vessels, increase the heart rate, increase the blood pressure, and raise the muscle tension. The first effects of amphetamine use are a general euphoria, a heightened level of activity, improved concentration, and a tendency to become very talkative. As the effects wear off, the user may go into a depression, which leads to even more drug use.

The effects of heavy amphetamine use sometimes produce the symptoms of paranoia—the drug takers fear that they are about to be arrested, that strange and awful things are happening to their bodies, that there are all sorts of horrible things about to kill or hurt them.

Some amphetamine users go on a drug-taking spree called a "run." During the run, they take the drug several times a day—some times continuously for up to six days. Because the drug is a stimulant and an appetite suppressant, the users do not sleep or eat while they are on a run. As a result, heavy amphetamine users are often undernourished and desperately in need of sleep.

A habitual user of amphetamines may develop both a physical and psychological dependence on the drug. When deprived of a supply, they have a very strong craving for the drug. Some also suffer withdrawal symptoms, which may include depression, cramps, sleepiness, apathy, irritability, and mental confusion.

Most users take amphetamines in pill form. Some, though, inject the drug in liquid form. When injected, the drug has a stronger effect than the same amount taken by mouth. It also builds up tolerance faster and produces more severe symptoms on withdrawal.

The most popular amphetamine for injecting is Methedrine (methamphetamine hydrochloride), which is known on the streets as "speed." Those who take speed frequently are known as "speed freaks."

Most speed freaks find it very hard to get along day-to-day and to function in society. They look and act like the stereotypes of "drug fiends," turning to lives of crime and violence to sustain their habit. Drug counselors say that the amphetamines are among the worst and most dangerous of all drugs.

AMT. See **AMPHETAMINES.**

AMYL NITRITE. A quick-acting inhalant that dilates the small blood vessels, lowers high blood pressure and relaxes the smooth (involuntary) muscles of the body. It takes effect within thirty seconds and lasts no more than about three minutes. Amyl nitrite is a clear yellow liquid that is usually sold in small glass vials that can be crushed with the fingers, allowing the vapor to escape.

The principal medical use of amyl nitrite is to relieve the pain of angina pectoris and to prevent seizures. Illicit users take the drug because of the belief that it is sexually stimulating and also for the distorted views of reality that it provides.

AMYTAL SODIUM. A barbiturate that is a frequent choice of drug abusers. After long-time, heavy use, the user suffers convulsions on stopping suddenly and experiences other severe withdrawal symptoms.

ANABOLIC STEROIDS. See **STEROIDS.**

ANALGESICS. A group of drugs that relieve pain without loss of consciousness. The word comes from the Greek, *an,* "without," *algesia,* "pain." Most analgesics, including aspirin, are abused, and analgesics used for pain relief are often combined with those used to get high.

ANESTHETICS. A class of drugs that do away with the feeling of pain. They are of two types: Local anesthetics that produce loss of sensation in just one part of the body and general anesthetics that affect the entire body and produce unconsciousness. Some illicit drugs, such as cocaine and the barbiturates, have anesthetic qualities.

ANGEL DUST. Slang for **PCP.**

ANILERIDINE. A synthetic compound similar to morphine and to meperdine. Trade names—Lerinol and Leritine. It has the same analgesic effect as morphine and can also have the same side effects, such as nausea and vomiting, faintness, and dizziness. An overdose can affect breathing and cause death.

ANTABUSE. Trade name for **DISULFIRAM.**

ANTIANXIETY TRANQUILIZERS. A group of drugs that are commonly prescribed to treat such complaints as anxiety, nervousness, tension, and stress. If taken in excessive amounts, the antianxiety tranquilizers can produce physical dependence and withdrawal symptoms similar to those associated with barbiturate withdrawal. Since these drugs, like alcohol or the barbiturates, produce euphoria and other pleasant effects, they are often chosen as drugs for abuse. Valium, Librium, Miltown, and Equanil are among the better-known trade names for antianxiety tranquilizers. These drugs usually are metabolized slowly by the body and lead to a slow-developing dependence and a prolonged and potentially dangerous withdrawal syndrome including seizures.

ANTIDEPRESSANTS. A group of prescription drugs used medically to elevate and improve mood in severely depressed patients. The antidepressants are rarely abused since they offer little pleasurable effect.

ANTIHISTAMINES. Drugs that block the action of histamine, a naturally occurring body compound that causes allergy-related symptoms, such as sneezing, itching, and runny nose. They are classified as nonbarbiturate sedative/hypnotics and when abused are mixed with alcohol or codeine to magnify the sedative effects. High doses of antihistamines can lead to excitation, restlessness, and convulsions. In the most severe cases, there is central nervous system depression and death from respiratory arrest.

ANTIPSYCHOTIC TRANQUILIZERS. A group of tranquilizer drugs used to treat the more serious forms of mental illness, those that are identified as psychoses. The drugs act to calm violent, hyperactive, and fearful patients. The antipsychotic tranquilizers have made it possible for many persons suffering with psychiatric disorders to leave the mental hospital and return to their homes and communities. Since these drugs do not produce euphoric or other pleasant effects, and sometimes produce very unpleasant side effects, they are not usually chosen as drugs of abuse. The antipsychotic tranquilizers do not cause physical dependence. Examples of these drugs include Thorazine, Mellaril, Trilafon, and Haldol.

ANXIETY. An emotional feeling of fear and apprehension that is not specifically related to a cause.

ANYWHERE. Slang for possessing or using drugs; sometimes specifically referring to marijuana.

ARMY DISEASE. Morphine addiction. The term arose after the Civil War when many soldiers were injected with morphine as an analgesic and developed an addiction to the drug. Although it started as a so-called "soldier's illness," morphine use spread widely in the postwar years until about 400,000, or about 1 percent of the population, was addicted.

ARTILLERY. Equipment for injecting narcotics. Usually includes a spoon to heat the drug and a hypodermic needle for the actual injection.

B

BABY. Slang for **MARIJUANA;** also a new, small heroin habit.

BACK UP. Allowing blood to enter the hypodermic needle as a way of ensuring that the tip of the needle is in a vein.

BACKWARDS. Slang for **BARBITURATES.** The name comes from the fact that barbiturates can reverse a panic reaction from LSD or another drug.

BAD SEED. Slang for **PEYOTE** or **MESCALINE.**

BAD TRIP. Slang for **PANIC REACTION.**

BAG. A quantity of either marijuana or heroin that is sold in paper or glassine envelopes or in plastic sandwich bags. The marijuana bags usually contain about one sixth of an ounce of the drug. They sell for $5 and are called "nickel bags." The nickel bag of heroin usually contains about five milligrams of the pure drug diluted with a white powder, such as milk sugar or quinine, so that it contains only about 3 percent heroin.

BAG LADY. A female seller of narcotics.

BAG MAN. A male seller of narcotics, though the term usually refers to the person who holds the money in drug transactions.

BALE. A fixed quantity, usually either a pound or a kilogram, of marijuana or another drug.

BALLOON EFFECT. Switching drugs when it becomes difficult or expensive to obtain the drug of choice. The term comes from the way inflated balloons change their shape when squeezed hard.

BALLOONS. Drugs, usually heroin, that are sold in rubber balloons so that in case of any danger of arrest the balloon can be swallowed.

BAM. Slang for **AMPHETAMINE.**

BAMBOO. Common name for an opium pipe.

BAMBU. A popular brand of cigarette paper used in rolling marijuana cigarettes.

BANG. To inject narcotics. The term is a play on the word "shoot."

BANK BANDITS. Slang for **BARBITURATES** or other sedative drugs.

BARBITAL. A long-acting barbiturate. Trade name—Veronal.

BARBITURATE. The largest and most common group of sedative/hypnotic drugs. They function by depressing the central nervous system. In small doses, the barbiturates relieve tension and anxiety without causing drowsiness. In large doses, they are hypnotics, or sleep inducers. When a large dose is not followed by sleep, though, it produces a pleasant, relaxed high, mental confusion, and sometimes stimulation, all of which are similar to the intoxicating effects of alcohol. In fact, some people call the barbiturates "solid alcohol." For this reason, barbiturates are often abused by those seeking alcohol's effects. In fact, alcohol is often taken along with the barbiturates, since the combination is even stronger than either of the single drugs.

The first barbiturate was developed in 1902 by two German chemists, Emil Fischer and Joseph von Mering. It was given the name Veronal, after the quiet, peaceful city in Italy where von Mering telegraphed news of the discovery to Fischer. Since then, over 2,500 barbiturates have been manufactured. Presently, only about 50 brands are available, and of those, only 12 are widely used.

The barbiturates are usually divided into three groups depending on how long they remain in the body. The long-lasting (6 to 24 hours) are phenobarbital (trade name—Luminal), barbital (Veronal), aprobarbital (Alurate), and Diallybarbituric acid (Dial). The short-to-intermediate acting (3 to 6 hours) are pentobarbital sodium (Nembutal), secobarbital sodium (Seconal), butabarbital sodium (Butisol Sodium), and amobarbital (Amytal). The one ultra-short acting (less than 3 hours) is thiopental soidum (Pentothal). (Because this last drug causes people to lose their inhibitions and to speak freely, it is sometimes used as a "truth serum," when people are being questioned by the police.)

The short-to-intermediate barbiturates are the most widely abused and the most dangerous. They are also the ones most frequently prescribed as sleeping pills to those who see a doctor about a sleep disturbance. These drugs are the most likely to produce intoxication, to be found on the illicit drug market, and to be used in suicide attempts. One of the most popular of the abused barbitals is a mixture of amobarbital and secobarbital known as tuinal.

Anyone who takes an overdose of a barbiturate develops the symptoms of severe shock—a weak, rapid pulse, cold, sweaty skin, and difficulty in breathing. The usual treatment, if detected early enough, is to pump out the stomach and administer artificial respiration. If untreated, there is a danger the abuser may die. In a more severe overdose, the kidneys stop functioning, breathing becomes even more difficult, and a coma and death follow.

Some users may develop dangerous delusions of persecution or of grandeur. For those who suffer from suicidal depression, the symptoms may become worse. Every year an estimated 5,000 Americans try to end their lives with overdoses of barbiturates.

The symptoms of withdrawal from barbiturate use are very severe. They resemble the delirium tremens that are frequently encountered by alcoholics undergoing withdrawal. Included are terrifying hallucinations, unstoppable shaking, a racing pulse, weakness, and fever, along with epileptic-like seizures.

Barbiturate addicts have great difficulty in functioning and closely resemble those suffering from severe alcoholism. They neglect their appearance, cannot hold a job, and alienate all their friends and family members. Their mood swings wildly from high elation to deep depression to hostile violence. Even within the drug community, barbiturate abusers are looked down on because they are so unattractive and so unpredictable.

Many of the slang words for the barbiturates are the colors of their various capsules or tablets, such as reds, blues, yellows, and pinks.

BARBS. Slang for **BARBITURATES.**

BASEBALL. Slang for **COCAINE FREEBASE.**

BASE HOUSE. A place where users indulge in a continual sale and use of cocaine freebase.

BEAST. Slang for **LSD.**

BEAT. To rob or cheat someone in a drug transaction.

BEE. A box or bag of marijuana.

BEER. An alcoholic beverage made by fermenting barley malt or other grains and adding the flavor of hops or other bitters. Most beers contain about 4 percent pure alcohol.

BEHIND. Taking a drug; "behind acid" means using LSD.

BELLADONNA. A sedative drug extracted from the plant, *Atropa belladonna*, which is also known as deadly night shade. In larger doses, belladonna can produce bizarre mental effects. In still larger doses, it is fatal.

BELLY HABIT. An addiction to narcotics. A reference to the stomach cramps that are among the withdrawal symptoms of ceasing narcotic use.

BELT. The pleasant high that follows drug use; the abuser "feels the belt."

BELTED. High on drugs.

BENNY. A Benzedrine pill.

BENT. The state of intoxication following drug use.

BENZ. Slang for **BENZEDRINE.**

BENZEDRINE. Trade name for amphetamine sulfate. A central nervous system stimulant, it was first synthesized in 1927 and found widespread use as an over-the-counter nasal inhaler and to supply extra energy and to counteract fatigue. Somehow, it was found that if the Benzedrine inhalers were opened and the amphetamine-soaked wick was dipped in water or coffee, the drink gave the user a terrific boost of energy.

BENZINE. A hydrocarbon similar to gasoline and kerosene that is obtained by distillation from petroleum. Widely used as a cleaning fluid, it is abused as an inhalant that has an intoxicating effect.

BENZODIAZEPINES. A group of chemicals used in the manufacture of four types of antianxiety tranquilizers: Chlordiazepoxide hydrochloride (Trade name—Librium); Diazepam (Valium); Oxazepam (Serax); and Chlorazepate dipotassium (Tranxene). The drugs are used mostly to treat mild attacks of anxiety and as muscle relaxants. Prolonged heavy use does produce a dependence, and withdrawal can lead to such symptoms as convulsions, depression, cramps, vomiting, agitation, and insomnia. See also **LIBRIUM, VALIUM, SERAX, TRANXENE.**

BERNIES. Slang for **COCAINE.**

BHANG. The name used in India for marijuana. Also the name of a drink made from the leaves and stem of the marijuana plant, to which milk, water, and pepper are added.

BIG BAG. A $10 bag of heroin.

BIG CHIEF. Slang for **MESCALINE.**

BIG D. Slang for LSD.

BIG MAN. A drug wholesaler, someone on a high level in the drug distribution network.

BING. An injection of narcotics. Also, solitary confinement while in prison.

BINGE. A short, intense period of alcohol or drug use.

BIPHETAMINE. A central nervous system stimulant containing two different amphetamines.

BIT. Either time spent in jail or one's favorite drug.

BIZ. The equipment used for preparing and injecting drugs.

BLACK BEAUTIES. Slang for either **AMPHETAMINES** or **BIPHETAMINES**.

BLACK GUNION. An especially powerful, dark-colored marijuana.

BLACK PILLS. Slang for **OPIUM.**

BLACK RUSSIAN. A very potent, dark-colored hashish that comes from Russia.

BLACK STUFF. Slang for **OPIUM.**

BLANK. Either an inert, nonnarcotic powder or a drug containing a high percentage of inert powder.

BLAST. Either to smoke marijuana or to feel the powerful effects of a drug.

BLAST PARTY. Several people coming together to smoke marijuana.

BLIND MUNCHIES. The very strong appetite or craving for any food, but especially sweets, that is felt after smoking marijuana.

BLOCK. A sale unit of drugs; the term, however, may be used to mean one kilogram (2.2 pounds) of marijuana or a small amount of narcotics (less than one ounce).

BLOCKBUSTERS. Slang for **BARBITURATES.**

BLOND. Golden-colored hashish from Lebanon or Morocco that is less potent than some of the darker varieties.

BLOTTER ACID. LSD soaked into a piece of blotting paper or heavy paper.

BLOW. Either to sniff cocaine or heroin, or to smoke marijuana.

BLOW A PILL. To smoke opium.

BLOW A STICK. To smoke a cigarette containing marijuana.

BLOW ONE'S MIND. To change one's state of mind and consciousness; to become intoxicated and lose mental control.

BLUE ACID. Slang for **LSD.**

BLUES. Slang for **AMYTAL SODIUM.** Also called Blue Birds, Blue Bullets, Blue Devils, Blue Dolls, Blue Heavens, Blue Jackets, Blue Tips, and Blue Velvet.

BLUE VELVET. Slang for **AMYTAL SODIUM.** Also a combination of drugs, such as a paregoric and an antihistamine, that have a sedative and mildly euphoric effect.

BODY DRUGS. Drugs, such as the opiates and barbiturates, that can lead to a physical dependence.

BOGART. Refusing or being slow to share a marijuana cigarette with others. The term comes from the dangling cigarette associated with movie actor Humphrey Bogart.

BOLSA. A bag of heroin.

BOMB. Either a very heavy, thick marijuana cigarette or a relatively pure sample of heroin.

BOMBED. High or intoxicated on a drug.

BOMBITA. Usually a combination of drugs, such as heroin, amphetamine, and barbiturate, that has a particularly strong effect.

BONITA. Milk sugar used to dilute heroin; sometimes a reference to the heroin itself.

BOOK. The *Physicians' Desk Reference,* an annual publication that describes all the commercial drugs being manufactured. Drug abusers use it to learn more about the drugs they are taking.

BOOTING. Slowly injecting heroin and allowing the blood-heroin mixture to back up into the syringe as a way of prolonging the highly pleasurable first effects of the drug.

BOSS. Either a very high quality drug or a very good, strong reaction to a drug.

BOUNCE POWDER. Slang for **COCAINE.**

BOXED. High or intoxicated on a drug.

BOY. Slang for **HEROIN.** (By way of contrast, one of the slang words for cocaine is "girl.")

BRAIN TICKLERS. Slang for either **BARBITURATES** or **AMPHETAMINES.**

BRICK. A pressed, one-kilogram block of marijuana that is ready to be shipped.

BRING DOWN. To calm and restore control to someone who is intoxicated or on a drug high.

BRITISH SYSTEM. The approach, favored in Great Britain, that allows doctors to prescribe certain illicit drugs as a means of preventing criminals from gaining control of the drug supply.

BRODY. Pretending to be sick or undergoing withdrawal in order to convince a doctor to prescribe drugs.

BROTHER. Slang for **HEROIN.**

BROWN. Heroin from Mexico that is brown in color because of the brown milk sugar that is added to the drug.

BROWNIES. Amphetamines that come in brown-colored capsules.

BROWN ROCK. Crystals of heroin used for smoking.

BROWN STUFF. Slang for **OPIUM,** as distinct from "white stuff," which is heroin.

BUFOTENINE. A hallucinogenic drug found in the skin of toads and in two plants, a mimosa, *Piptadenia peregrina,* and a mushroom, *Amanita muscaria* or fly agaric. The drug causes color hallucinations, confused time and space perception, and mental impairment.

BUM BEND. A bad reaction to LSD or other drugs.

BUMMER. A bad experience that may or may not be caused by drugs.

BUM TRIP. A bad, panic reaction to a drug, usually a hallucinogen.

BUNDLE. A stack of 25 five-dollar bags of heroin held together by a rubber band. The drug is delivered this way to the pushers, who then separate the bags for sale on the street.

BUNK HABIT. Either smoking opium or hanging around a room where opium is being smoked to inhale the fumes. The bunk is the couch on which the opium smokers recline.

BURESE. Slang for **COCAINE.**

BURN. To cheat or be cheated in a drug transaction.

BURN ARTIST. Someone who cheats in drug transactions.

BURNED. To be cheated in a drug transaction. Also, to be identified as a police officer.

BURNED OUT. A condition of long-time drug abusers, usually nonnarcotic, who are unable to function in society. Also, stopping drug use by a chronic abuser.

BUSH. Slang for **MARIJUANA.**

BUSINESSMAN'S LUNCH. Slang for either **AMPHETA-MINES** or **DMT.** The term is used because these drugs have short-lasting effects.

BUST. To arrest.

BUTISOL SODIUM. Trade name for butabarbital sodium, an intermediate-acting barbiturate.

BUTTON. Slang for **PEYOTE.**

BUY. To purchase a drug. The common expression is to "make a buy."

BUZZ. The high, euphoric feeling that comes with drug use.

C

C. Slang for **COCAINE.**

CABALLO. Slang for **HEROIN.**

CA-CA. Slang word for counterfeit or highly-adulterated heroin.

CACHE. Hiding place for drugs.

CACTUS. Slang for **PEYOTE.**

CADET. An inexperienced drug user.

CAFFEINE. A mild stimulant found naturally in coffee, tea, and cocoa and added to many foods and soft drinks to enhance the flavor. The substance works on the central nervous system.

Habitual, heavy consumers of caffeine can develop a dependency. Excessive intake of caffeine can cause nervousness, insomnia, headache, and dizziness.

CAN. One ounce of marijuana.

CANADA BLACK. A dark-colored marijuana grown in Canada.

C AND H. A mixture of cocaine and heroin.

C AND M. A mixture of cocaine and morphine.

CANCELED STICK. An ordinary cigarette from which the tobacco has been removed and replaced with marijuana.

CANDY. A general term for drugs.

CANDY MAN. A seller of drugs.

CANNABIDIOL. A drug found in marijuana that is believed not to have any psychological effects.

CANNABIS. A group of drugs derived from plants of that name – *Cannabis sativa, Cannabis indica,* and *Cannabis ruderalis.* The drugs are made from the leaves and flowers of the plants, which contain the active ingredient tetrahydrocannabinol (THC). *C. indica* produces the biggest quantity and the most potent THC; *C. ruderalis* produces the least. The stems of the Cannabis plants are made into hemp for rope and twine. The seeds are used as food, and oil pressed from the seeds is used to make paint.

The effects of taking a cannabis drug vary considerably, depending on the users, where they take it, and what they expect. The effects include stimulant, depressant, and hallucinogenic reactions.

CANNED GOODS. A general term for any drugs.

CAP. To buy drugs.

CARBONA. A brand of cleaning fluid that is inhaled, making the user feel delirious.

CARBON TETRACHLORIDE. A cleaning fluid that produces intoxication when its fumes are inhaled. The fluid and the vapor can irritate the skin and eyes. Large doses of the drug can cause headache, mental confusion, depression, fatigue, nausea, and vomiting. In extreme cases it can lead to death.

CARRY. To have drugs in one's possession.

CARTWHEELS. Slang for **AMPHETAMINES.**

CAT. A man or, more specifically, a member of a particular group.

CATECHOLAINES. A group of chemicals made in the body, including epinephrine, norepinephrine, and dopamine. It is believed that some drugs produce their effects because of their similarity to these chemicals.

CATNIP. A strong-smelling herb that is sometimes sold as marijuana and sometimes added to marijuana. Some believe it has hallucinogenic effects.

CB. Slang for **DORIDEN.** The term comes from the manufacturer's name, Ciba.

CENT. Slang for one dollar.

CENTRAL NERVOUS SYSTEM. The brain and spinal cord, the body system most affected by psychoactive drugs.

CHALK. Slang for **AMPHETAMINES,** although the term is also sometimes used for **COCAINE.**

CHANDOO. Opium that is to be used for smoking.

CHANNEL. A vein used for injecting narcotics; also a source of drugs.

CHARAS. Indian word for hashish.

CHARGE. The sudden euphoria on taking a drug, particularly an opiate. Also, a marijuana cigarette.

CHARLES, CHARLIE, CHARLEY. Slang for **COCAINE.**

CHASING THE BAG. Seeking the very best heroin available.

CHASING THE DRAGON. Heating a mixture of heroin and barbiturate and inhaling the fumes through a small paper tube. Since the heated mixture looks like a small dragon and slides about, the abuser "chases the dragon" to get all the fumes.

CHICAGO GREEN. Green-colored potent marijuana.

CHICHARRA. A cigarette containing marijuana and tobacco that is passed around from smoker to smoker.

CHICK. Slang for **COCAINE.**

CHILL. To refuse to sell drugs to someone.

CHILLUM. A cone-shaped, clay pipe with a short, straight stem that is used for smoking marijuana. The smoke comes out from the bottom of the cone and is inhaled with the help of a cupped hand.

CHINA WHITE. Very powerful heroin that is white in color. Also, the street name for alpha-methyfentanyl, a very potent synthetic, narcotic, analgesic drug that is at least 100 times stronger than morphine.

CHIPPING. Occasional drug use, not enough to develop an addiction.

CHLORAL HYDRATE. Trichloroacetaldehyde, a nonbarbiturate sedative/hypnotic, the first sleep-inducing drug. When combined with alcohol it produces extreme intoxication and is called either a Mickey Finn or a Knockout Drop. Long-time use can lead to physical and psychological dependence and withdrawal symptoms on stopping.

CHLORAZEPATE DIPOTASSIUM. An antianxiety tranquilizer that is sold under the trade name Tranxene.

CHLORDIAZEPOXIDE. An antianxiety tranquilizer that is sold under the trade name Librium.

CHLOROFORM. An anesthetic that, when inhaled in small amounts, can produce an alcohol-like intoxication.

CHLORPROMAZINE. An antipsychotic tranquilizer used for reducing the patient's fears, hostility, and anxieties in severe mental illness. Trade name—Thorazine.

CHRONIC. Long lasting.

CHRISTMAS TREES. Capsules containing a mixture of amphetamines and barbiturates.

CHUCK HABIT. An overwhelming appetite following withdrawal from narcotic use.

CLEAN. Not carrying or using drugs. Also, to remove the seeds and stems from marijuana plants.

CLEAR UP. To stop abusing drugs.

CLIP. A pincer-like device used to hold the short butt of a burning marijuana cigarette.

COASTING. Feeling euphoric after drug use.

COCA. A tree, scientific name *Erythroxylon coca*, that grows wild in the valleys of the Andes Mountains in Bolivia and Peru and is the source of cocaine. The coca tree grows as tall as six feet and is covered with shiny, oval-shaped, greenish-brown leaves from which the cocaine is extracted. For at least 2,000 years, the Indians of South America have chewed the coca leaves as a stimulant—getting extra strength and energy, warding off the cold of the mountains, reducing their appetites, and treating a wide variety of diseases. An estimated 90 percent of the Indians chew coca leaves, which can be compared to coffee or tea drinking habits in the western world. (The coca plant should not be confused with the cocoa plant, which is the source of cocoa and chocolate.)

COCAINE. A major stimulant with strong energizing effects that last only a short while.

The leaves of the coca tree, the source of cocaine, has been chewed by perhaps 90 percent of all the Indians in Peru and Bolivia for some 2,000 years. Cocaine was no problem to them, however, since the drug entered their stomachs where acids neutralized the full effect. No one became addicted; no one died.

When it was first isolated in the 1850s, cocaine was considered a wonder drug. It was a very effective pain killer and was used in surgery of the eye, nose, and throat, since it provided anesthesia and prevented bleeding. Sigmund Freud recommended it to relieve depression and fatigue, to control asthma and digestive disorders, and to treat addictions to alcohol or morphine. Further, the first recipe for Coca-Cola included cocaine, which stayed in the popular soft drink from 1886 until 1903.

The dangers of the drug became obvious early in this century when users discovered that injecting or snorting pure cocaine increased its power. A mild overdose of cocaine causes such symptoms as irritability, anxiety, and mental confusion. Long-term chronic use can produce depression and irrational fears that there are harmful people about to attack. A frequent symptom are the so-called "cocaine bugs," imaginary creatures crawling on the skin. A more severe overdose can lead to dizziness, tremors, hostility, panic reactions, chest pains, heart palpitations, vomiting, stomach pains, and convulsions. At extremely high levels, the cocaine can depress parts of the brain, causing the heart and breathing to stop.

Most cocaine sold on the street is sniffed or snorted up through the nose. The user puts some of the powder on a clean, dry surface, like a mirror, and uses a razor blade to chop it into a finer powder and arrange it in a line. Then, using either a straw or a rolled up dollar bill, the user breathes in the cocaine.

Another, less popular way of taking cocaine is by injection. The user dissolves the powder in water and injects the liquid in a vein in his or her arm.

Of all the illicit drugs, cocaine is currently the most popular drug of choice. Once closely associated with the rich and the powerful and with the stars of the entertainment and sports worlds, cocaine is now used by people of all ages, all backgrounds, and all levels of income. An addictive drug, cocaine leads to both physical and psychological dependency.

COCAINE ANONYMOUS. A self-help organization for cocaine patterned on the older Alcoholics Anonymous. The group holds regular meetings at which the members relate their experiences—successes and failures—as they try to break their dependency.

COCAINE FREEBASE. A much stronger, more purified form of cocaine. Freebase is also suitable for smoking, while the usual form of cocaine is not. It is usually prepared from ordinary cocaine by the users, not the dealers.

To make freebase, the users add water and ammonium hydroxide to separate the cocaine hydrochloride from coca. The freebase is then mixed in a fast-drying solvent, such as ether. After the ether evaporates, the substance that is left is pure cocaine freebase.

Users often try to speed up the evaporation process by heating the mixture. Because ether is highly flammable, this is extremely dangerous. It has caused many serious accidents, including fires and explosions.

Freebase cannot be dissolved in water. Therefore it cannot be sniffed or injected. It can only be taken by smoking. Users smoke freebase in a special water pipe. The bowl has several layers of stainless steel screens. The freebase is placed on the top screen. As the pipe is heated, the substance melts and gives off vapors, which the user inhales.

The result is a sudden and intense high as the fumes are quickly absorbed by the lungs and reach the brain a few seconds later. But the euphoria only lasts for about two minutes before the feeling changes to one of restless irritability. This state is so uncomfortable that freebase smokers continue smoking either until they collapse or until they run out of the drug.

CODEINE. A mild opiate, methylmorphine, found in opium. Classified as a narcotic, it has the same analgesic effect as morphine, but is only one-sixth to one-tenth as strong. Its main medical uses are as a pain reliever and cough suppressant. In large doses it can have a stimulant effect. Codeine addiction is rare; the abuser, though, does suffer from comparatively mild symptoms of withdrawal.

COFFEE. A stimulant beverage that contains 2 percent caffeine.

COKE. Slang for **COCAINE.**

COKE HEAD. A cocaine addict.

COLD SHOT. The sale of a counterfeit drug or the injection of such a drug.

COLD TURKEY. The sudden and complete withdrawal from heavy narcotic use, either because of being hospitalized or imprisoned or because of the inability to buy more of the drug for lack of money or loss of contact with a dealer. The name comes from the gooseflesh that is one of the symptoms of withdrawal.

COLLAPSED VEIN. A condition, common among long-time heroin users, caused by frequent injections in that vein, contaminants in the heroin, or unsterile needles. After a vein has become so weak that the heroin cannot be injected into it, the user starts on a new vein—one in the arm, leg, hand, neck, or foot. When there are no more usuable veins, the abuser may switch to subcutaneous, under the skin, injections.

COLLAR. An arrest.

COLOMBIAN. Marijuana that comes from Colombia, usually of a very high quality.

COLOMBIAN GOLD, COLOMBIAN RED. Two varieties of marijuana from Colombia, identified by the color of the leaves.

COMA. A state of prolonged unconsciousness from which it is difficult or impossible to rouse the person.

COME DOWN. To return to a normal state after the effects of a drug have worn off.

COMPULSIVE DRUG USE. A classification, defined by the National Commission on Marijuana and Drug Abuse, that involves frequent, heavy drug use over a long period of time, producing a dependency that cannot be discontinued without experiencing withdrawal symptoms. It is believed that such drug use comes from the individual's need for a sense of security, comfort, or relief from anxiety and tension.

CONNECT. Either to find a source of drugs or to buy drugs.

CONNECTION. Someone who sells drugs.

CONTACT. Someone who can supply drugs.

CONTACT HIGH. Getting high either by breathing marijuana smoke exhaled by others or by being with others doing drugs whose mood and behavior is picked up by the nondrug user.

CONTROLLED SUBSTANCES ACT OF 1970. The act sets up five classifications, or "schedules," of drugs of abuse.
  I. Heroin, marijuana, LSD. High potential for abuse and no known medical use.
  II. Morphine, methadone, amphetamines. Same as Schedule I, but with some accepted medical uses.
  III. Barbiturates. Some potential for abuse and few regulations on medical use.
  IV. Long-acting barbiturates and antianxiety tranquilizers. Less potential for abuse and fewer regulations on medical use.
  V. Cough medicines with codeine. Minimal potential for abuse and virtually no regulation on medical use.
The illicit sale of Schedule I or II drugs has a maximum penalty of fifteen years imprisonment and a $25,000 fine. The illicit sale of Schedule III, IV, or V drugs has a maximum penalty of one year imprisonment and a $5,000 fine.

COOK. To heat a mixture of heroin and water in a spoon or bottle top until the heroin powder has dissolved and can be injected. Also refers to heating a mixture of cocaine with water and ammonia hydroxide to produce freebase. See **COCAINE FREEBASE.**

COOKER. The spoon or bottle top used to prepare heroin for injection, or paraphernalia used to prepare cocaine freebase.

COOL. Smart, in control, safe, not overly involved.

COP. Either a police officer or to buy drugs.

COPILOT. Someone who is with drug takers, but does not take drugs, in order to care for those who have bad drug reactions.

COPILOTS. Slang for **AMPHETAMINES.**

COP MAN. A drug seller.

COTTON. A small bit of cotton used as a filter through which prepared heroin is drawn into a hypodermic needle.

COTTON HABIT. Irregular use of narcotics or sharing narcotics with others because of a lack of supply.

COTTON SHOOTER. A desperate narcotics addict who soaks out the heroin remaining in cotton used as a filter and injects that substance.

COURAGE PILLS. Slang for **BARBITURATES.**

CRACK. A very potent form of cocaine freebase. It is sold in small, clear-plastic vials with colorful lids that look like vitamin capsules. The crack itself is small chunks or crystals that are light-colored. There are usually three small pieces, called "rocks," in a vial.

Crack does not burn. To give off its vapors, it must be heated to a high temperature. Some users break the rocks into tiny bits and sprinkle them on tobacco or marijuana cigarettes and inhale the vapors when smoking the cigarette. Most others place the rocks on a fine steel screen in a water pipe, heat the pipe with a small, hand-held gas heater, and inhale the fumes.

The crack vapor goes right to the lungs and passes into the bloodstream and to the brain within seconds. The user immediately gets the special high that crack brings.

Crack can be bought in small amounts. The usual price is about $10 a vial, though the cost varies from about $5 to over $200. A vial contains about 300 milligrams of crack, which is enough for two "hits" or "fixes."

Crack is prepared by the dealers by mixing cocaine, water, and baking soda to make a thick paste. They then heat the paste and allow it to dry. When dried it looks like a rough, slightly-dirty bar of soap. Finally, the dealers break the crack into small chunks and place them in the vials.

Even though crack first appeared in 1985, it has rapidly become one of the most widely used, and abused, of all drugs. It is cheap. It is fast acting. It is easily available. It very quickly leads to addiction. And it is much more powerful than any other form of cocaine.

Since crack use has become widespread, police are reporting a rising number of cases of violent and unpredictable behavior among drug abusers. Burglaries and armed robberies are up in areas where crack is sold because these are the crimes that give users enough cash for a quick fix. Every kind of crime from shoplifting, credit-card scams, prostitution, passing bad checks, embezzlement, and petty thievery to murder is common among people who deal or use crack. The slang terms for crack include rock. See **COCAINE** and **ROCKS.**

CRANK. Slang for **AMPHETAMINE.**

CRANK BUGS. Hallucinations of bugs crawling over the skin after amphetamine use.

CRAP. Low-quality, highly-diluted heroin.

CRASH. The uncomfortable feelings of drowsiness and despondency that may follow a drug-induced high.

CRATER. A large abscess, or collection of pus, in the skin caused by frequent injections of a drug at that spot.

CREEP. An addict who begs or takes a demeaning job in order to get drugs, instead of stealing or obtaining the drugs in a riskier way.

CRIB. One's home or apartment or where one goes to inject drugs.

CROAKER. A doctor.

CROSSROADS. Slang for **AMPHETAMINES.**

CROSS-TOLERANCE. A condition in which tolerance to one drug results in a tolerance to a similar drug. For example, someone who takes large doses of heroin will feel no effect from a smaller dose of methadone.

CRYSTAL. Slang for **PCP** and some **AMPHETAMINES.**

CRYSTAL PALACE. A place where methedrine users come together.

CUBE. Slang for **LSD.**

CUT. To add material to a drug to increase its bulk.

CYCLAZOCINE. A narcotic antagonist used to treat addicts. Cyclazocine reduces the effect of heroin, which makes it easier for the addict to break the heroin habit. Since the cyclazocine produces pleasant feelings, addicts are motivated to continue. Eventual withdrawal from cyclazocine produces only very mild symptoms.

D

D. Slang for **DORIDEN.**

DABBLING. Using narcotics moderately and occasionally.

DAGGA. South African term for marijuana.

DALMANE. A nonbarbiturate sedative useful in treating insomnia. It can caused blurred vision, confusion, and staggering. Dalmane is chemically related to Benzodiazepines, such as Valium.

DALMAZOL. A drug that turns into Valium in the stomach. See also **VALIUM.**

DARVON. Trade name for propoxyphene hydrochloride, a narcotic pain reliever related to methadone. It is now found to be addicting, even though it was originally thought to be nonaddictive. Low dosages can cause feelings of euphoria, along with drowsiness and impaired driving skills. Overdosage can lead to convulsions, failure of the breathing and blood systems, coma, and even death.

DATURA. A narcotic and hallucinogenic drug made from the plant, *Datura stramonium.* Often mixed either with hashish or beer to produce severe intoxication and mental confusion.

DEA. See **DRUG ENFORCEMENT ADMINISTRATION.**

DEALER. Someone who sells drugs. Sometimes a dealer is one who sells "soft" drugs like marijuana, whereas a pusher sells "hard" drugs like heroin.

DEALER'S BAND. A rubber band used to hold packets of heroin on the wrist of the dealer. The band is attached so that, if a police officer is seen, the heroin can quickly be flipped away.

DECK. A small packet of heroin or a pack of marijuana cigarettes.

DECRIMINALIZATION. Proposed changes in the drug laws so that possession of small amounts of some drugs for personal use will not be treated as a criminal offense, with the possibility of a prison term, but as a civil offense, with the possibility of only a fine.

DEEDA. Slang for **LSD.**

DELIRIANTS. Any substance that produces delirium, delusions, or hallucinations. Most of the deliriants are inhalants, including chloroform, nitrous oxide, ether, glue, gasoline, carbon tetrachloride, benzine, paint thinner, nail polish and nail polish remover, and many spray-can preparations.

DELIRIUM TREMENS. A serious mental and physical condition that characterizes the last stage of withdrawal from alcohol. Among the symptoms are nausea and vomiting, frightening hallucinations, weakness, tremulousness, and possibly collapse.

DELYSD. A trade name for **LSD.**

DEMEROL. The trade name of a synthetic narcotic, meperdine hydrochloride, that is widely used medically as an analgesic and sedative. Although it may not cause a physical dependency, there is a clear danger of addiction.

DEPENDENCE. Condition that results from continuing drug use. Physical dependence occurs when the body adapts to the drug so that there is a physical reaction on withdrawal. Psychological dependence occurs when the individual craves the satisfaction and feeling of wellbeing the drug brings, but does not feel a strong, physical need for the drug. On stopping, the user does feel mental discomfort. Most dependence is both physical and psychological.

DEPRESSANT. Any drug that reduces the activity of bodily organs, especially the brain. Depressants are the most common of all drug types and include alcohol, barbiturates, tranquilizers, and inhalants, among others. With increasing dosage, the effects of depressants go from relaxation to sedation, sleep, and anesthesia, to coma, and even death. When depressants are combined, their effect is vastly increased, as is the danger of death.

DESBUTAL. Trade name for a combination drug containing an amphetamine (methamphetamine) and a barbiturate (pentobarbital). The drug was developed as an aid to dieting, the amphetamine depressing the appetite and the barbiturate reducing the amphetamine's side effects, such as nervousness and insomnia. Heavy and frequent usage, however, may lead to dependence and severe withdrawal symptoms.

DESIGNER DRUGS. A number of laboratory-made drugs that are similar to, but not exactly like, illegal substances, and are just as dangerous. One notable example is Ecstasy, or **MDMA.**

DESERPIDINE. A major tranquilizer found in *Rauwolfia serpentina,* the so-called snakeroot plant. Trade names—Harmonyl, Enduronyl, Oreticyl.

DESIPRAMINE HYDROCHLORIDE. An antidepressant drug. Trade names—Pertofrane, Norpramin.

DESOXYN. Trade name for the central nervous system stimulant, methamphetamine hydrochloride, that is recommended for short-term dieting.

DETOXIFICATION. A program that provides guidance and help to individuals to break their drug habits.

DEXAMYL. A central nervous system stimulant recommended for short-term dieting. It contains an amphetamine (dextroam-phetamine sulfate) to suppress the appetite and a barbiturate (amobarbital) to dampen any over-stimulation by the amphetamine. Long-time use may result in a dependency, and overdose may lead either to over-stimulation or excessive mood depression.

DEXEDRINE. Trade name for dextroamphetamine, a central nerv-ous system stimulant that is about twice as potent as the other amphetamines. Used in dieting, as mood elevator for minor depres-sion, and to treat alcoholism and narcolepsy (involuntary sleep).

DEXIES. Slang for **DEXEDRINE.**

DEXTROAMPHETAMINE. Chemical name for **DEXEDRINE.**

DEXTROMORAMIDE. A synthetic narcotic analgesic, trade name—Palfium. It is a more potent analgesic than morphine and has milder withdrawal symptoms.

DIACETYLMORPHINE. Chemical name for **HEROIN.**

DIAZEPAM. An antianxiety tranquilizer and muscle relaxant. Trade name—Valium.

DIHYDROCODEINE. A drug derived from morphine that is twice as potent an analgesic as codeine. It is used in cough medicines and for controlling minor pains. Heavy use can result in dependency and withdrawal symptoms.

DILAUDID. Trade name for hydromorphone hydrochloride, an analgesic derived from morphine that is even more potent than morphine and with fewer side effects, although lasting for a shorter time. The withdrawal reactions after habitual use are similar to those for morphine.

DILOCOL. A cough syrup containg hydromorphone hydrochloride plus other ingredients. See **DILAUDID.**

DIME. Slang word for $10.

DIP and DAB. To use heroin occasionally.

DIPHENHYDRAMINE. An antianxiety tranquilizer, trade name— Benadryl.

DIRTY. Carrying or using narcotics or marijuana containing seeds, stems, and twigs.

DIRTY URINE. A sample of urine taken for testing and found to show traces of drugs.

DISTILLED SPIRITS. Alcoholic beverages made by distillation, such as whisky, brandy, rum, gin, and vodka. The alcohol component varies between 25 and 50 percent and higher.

DISULFIRAM. A drug used to help alcoholics break the habit. If alcohol is taken within five days of taking disulfiram, the alcoholic may experience great discomfort, including headaches, vomiting, difficulty in breathing, palpitations, and dizziness. Trade name— Antabuse.

DITRAN. Trade name for piperidyl benzilate, a hallucinogenic drug. It causes intoxication, mental disorganization, disorientation of time, place, color, form, and distance. Although there are no visual hallucinations, the user loses touch with reality.

DMT. Short for dimethyltryptamine, a hallucinogenic drug similar to psilocybin. Parsley or some other plant is soaked in the DMT, dried, and then smoked, producing effects similar to LSD. Its effects start within two minutes and last for under an hour.

DO. A slang word for taking drugs.

DOGIE. Slang for **HEROIN.**

DOLLAR. One hundred dollars.

DOLLIES. Slang for **DOLOPHINE.**

DOLOPHINE. Trade name for methadone hydrochloride. It was developed in Germany during World War II as a substitute for morphine and heroin and was named after the German dictator, Adolf Hitler. Dolophine is a synthetic opiate analgesic that is slightly more potent than morphine, but its withdrawal symptoms are very much milder. See **METHADONE.**

DOM. A very strong hallucinogen that is better known as STP.

DOPE. Originally any narcotic, now a reference to all drugs.

DOPE FIEND. Originally a narcotics addict or society's description of a narcotics addict, now used sarcastically by drug abusers to describe themselves.

DORIDEN. Trade name for glutethimide, a nonbarbiturate sedative/hypnotic that works like short-acting barbiturates. Users quickly develop a tolerance for the drug and suffer severe withdrawal symptoms, including death in about 20 percent of the cases.

DOSE. Slang for **LSD.**

DOUBLE TROUBLE. A combination of drugs, such as two barbiturates or a barbiturate and an amphetamine. Also refers to special self-help groups of Alcoholics Anonymous whose members also have a psychiatric disorder such as depression or manic depressive illness and may be on a medication for treatment.

DO UP. To inject heroin.

DOWN. Either a bad reaction to a drug or the return to normal after a drug high.

DOWNER. Either a drug, such as a barbiturate or tranquilizer, that acts as a depressant or any unpleasant experience.

DR. FEELGOOD. A physician willing to give drug users prescriptions for illicit drugs.

DRAG. Either a deep inhalation of a tobacco or marijuana cigarette, a bad drug experience, or anything dull or unpleasant.

DRAGGED. A panic reaction that sometimes follows smoking marijuana.

DREAMER. Someone who uses morphine; sometimes a reference to the drug itself.

DRIVERS. Slang for **AMPHETAMINES.**

DROP. To take a drug by mouth.

DROPPER. A medicine dropper used to inject heroin. In practice, the needle is attached to the tip of the dropper. The rubber bulb acts as the plunger, or syringe, forcing the drug out through the needle and into the vein.

DRUG. Any natural or man-made substance that changes function or structure in a living being. More commonly, it is a nonfood chemical that alters the mood of the user. While most people reserve the term for illicit substances, such substances as alcohol, tobacco, coffee, and tea, are also drugs. The medicines prescribed by doctors are drugs as well. Drugs can be in any form—powder, liquid, solid, gas, or plant material.

DRUG ABUSE. The nonmedical use of a drug that adversely affects the health and well-being of the user and has a negative impact on others. The definition of the American Medical Association adds that the drug be taken "in large doses that may lead to psychological dependency, tolerance, and abnormal behavior."

DRUG ADDICT. Originally a habitual narcotics user, now extended to anyone who is a regular user of mood-changing drugs.

DRUG ENFORCEMENT ADMINISTRATION. The main federal agency enforcing the drug laws. Created in 1973, its task is to bring to justice all individuals and organizations that grow, manufacture, or distribute controlled substances.

DRUG LORDS. The operators of big drug rings who provide the capital for the drug trade.

DRUNK. In a state of intoxication. Originally only used for people intoxicated with alcohol, but now extended to drug-induced intoxication. Its main symptoms are mental confusion and lack of physical control.

DRY. Not using drugs, either permanently or temporarily.

DUMMY. An inert white powder, such as talcum, quinine, or scouring powder, that is either added to heroin or sold as heroin.

DUSTER. A tobacco or marijuana cigarette to which either heroin or PCP has been added.

DYNAMITE. Any very strong drug or a combination of cocaine and heroin.

DYNO. Very pure, high-quality heroin.

EAR RINGS. Ringing in the ears after smoking cocaine freebase.

EATER. Someone who swallows drugs.

ECSTASY. Slang for **MDMA** (methylenedioxymethamphetamine). A combination of a hallucinogen and methamphetamine, a stimulant.

ELAVIL. An antidepressant that appears to have little effect on normal mood states.

ELECTRIC KOOL-ADE. A sweet punch drink to which LSD has been added.

ELEPHANT. Slang for **PCP** because of its legal use as an animal anesthetic.

EMBROIDERY. Scars left on the skin by frequent drug injections.

EQUANIL. Trade name for meprobamate, an antianxiety tranquilizer and nonhypnotic muscle relaxant. Large doses produce a state similar to barbiturate intoxication and can lead to severe withdrawal symptoms.

ERGOGENICS. Another word for stimulants.

ERGOT. A fungus that grows on rye, *Claviceps purpurea,* that is used to treat migraine headaches, depression in the elderly, and to induce labor in expectant mothers. Can cause some mental confusion.

ETHCHLORVYNOL. A nonbarbiturate sedative/hypnotic that produces effects like those of a short-acting barbiturate. Long- time heavy use can create physical and psychological dependence and severe withdrawal reactions. Trade name—Placidyl.

ETHER. A light highly-flammable liquid that is used as a general anesthetic and as a solvent in making cocaine freebase. Inhaling the vapor or drinking a few drops in water or alcohol produces an intoxication similar to that of alcohol.

ETHINAMATE. A nonbarbiturate sedative/hypnotic with the trade name Valmid. In action it is similar to short-acting barbiturates. Long-term, heavy use can lead to dependency, and stopping suddenly can bring on withdrawal symptoms.

EUPHORIA. A sense of extreme happiness, pleasure, and joy. Many drugs are taken to experience this state.

EYE OPENER. The first drug taken on a particular day.

F

FACTORY. Either the place where drugs are manufactured or prepared for sale or the equipment used for injecting narcotics.

FAKE A BLAST. To pretend to be under the influence of a drug.

FALLING OUT. Drifting into sleep while or after taking a drug.

FALSE POSITIVE. A drug test that, by mistake, shows the presence of a drug when the subject had not been taking any drugs. False negative is the exact opposite—a test result showing no drugs when, in fact, the subject had been taking drugs.

FATTY. A thick marijuana cigarette.

FEELING THE HABIT. The start of withdrawal symptoms.

FIEND. A drug addict who cannot control his or her habit.

FINGER. Hashish, usually from the Mediterranean region, that is packed in finger-sized sticks. Also, a condom filled with a drug and either hidden in the rectum or swallowed.

FIVE-CENT BAG. Five dollars worth of drugs.

FIVES. Tablets containing five milligrams of a drug, usually an amphetamine.

FIX. An injection of a drug or a single dose of a drug.

FLAKE. Slang for **COCAINE.**

FLAKY. Being somewhat strange or crazy, as if under the influence of a drug.

FLASH. The sudden rush of euphoric good feelings that immediately follow drug use.

FLASHBACK. Hallucinatory sensations experienced some time after the effects of a hallucinatory drug have worn off. Most flashbacks are visual, although they may affect any of the senses. The flashbacks may be pleasant or terrifying.

FLEA POWDER. Low quality or highly-diluted heroin or other narcotic.

FLIP. To have either a bad, panic reaction to a drug or to have a very pleasant mood change as the result of drug use.

FLOATING. Feeling high and light-headed on a drug.

FLOWERS. The flowers of the marijuana plant.

FLUFF. To add bulk to heroin or cocaine by chopping it up to a finer consistency, filtering the drug through a stocking, or by adding powder that has no chemical effect.

FLUPHENAZINE HYDROCHLORIDE. An antipsychotic tranquilizer, trade names—Proloxin and Permitil.

FLURAZEPAM HYDROCHLORIDE. A minor tranquilizer, trade name—Dalmane.

FLUSH. Same as **FLASH.**

FLY AGARIC. A hallucinogenic, poisonous mushroom, *Amanita muscaria,* that grows in North America, Europe, and parts of northern Asia. In small amounts, it causes intoxication, hallucinations, euphoria, and distorted perception. Larger doses cause vomiting, diarrhea, and exremely rapid breathing. Very large doses quickly lead to delirium, convulsions, coma, and death.

FLYING. Same as **FLOATING.**

FLYING SAUCERS. The hallucinogenic seeds of a variety of morning glory plants with that trade name.

FOLD UP. To stop using or selling drugs.

FOOTBALLS. Certain pills, such as diphetamine and Dilaudid, that are manufactured in that shape.

FORWARDS. Slang for **AMPHETAMINES.**

FOURS. Tylenol pills that contain codeine. The name comes from the fact that the pills are numbered four to show their strength.

FREAK. A heavy drug user whose behavior and appearance is strange and bizarre.

FREAK OUT. To hallucinate or to have a strong, unpleasant reaction to a drug.

FREEBASE. See **COCAINE FREEBASE.**

FREEZE. To refuse to sell drugs to someone trying to make a purchase.

FRISCO SPEEDBALL. A mixture of heroin and cocaine, some times with the addition of LSD.

FRONT. To pay for drugs in advance.

FRUIT SALAD. Taking a variety of pills without knowing what they are. Sometimes this is done by selecting pills from a collection of different, unidentified pills. Sometimes people just take pills from every bottle in the family medicine chest.

FULL MOON. Either the round top part of the peyote or a round cake of hashish.

FUN. A measure of opium.

FUZZ. An officer of the law.

G

GAGE. Slang for **MARIJUANA.**

GAMMON. One microgram, which equals one-millionth of a gram.

GANGA. Slang for **MARIJUANA.**

GANGSTER. Slang for **MARIJUANA.**

GANJA. Name in India and Jamaica for marijuana.

GAPING. A reference to the frequent yawning of people withdrawing from a narcotic habit.

GARBAGE. Drugs that are either of poor quality or highly-diluted.

GARBAGE HEAD. Someone who will take any drug to get high.

GASOLINE. The fuel that, when its fumes are inhaled, produces a deliriant effect.

GAUGE. Slang for **MARIJUANA.**

G.B. Short for goof balls, which is slang for **BARBITURATES.**

GEE. Slang for **OPIUM.**

GEEZE. Either a narcotic or an injection of a narcotic.

GERONIMO. An alcohol drink, usually wine, with a barbiturate dissolved.

GET DOWN. Either to smoke marijuana or to inject heroin.

GET OFF. To feel the effects of a drug.

GET THE YEN OFF. To satisfy one's craving for a drug.

GHOST. Slang for **LSD.**

GIGGLE WEED. Slang for **MARIJUANA.**

GIMMICK. The equipment used for injecting a drug.

GIRL. Slang for **COCAINE.**

GLOW. A drug-caused high or euphoria.

GLUE SNIFFING. Inhaling the fumes from a glue, such as model-airplane glue, that contains toluene and that has an intoxicant or deliriant effect. Glue sniffing is becoming less popular, (1) because it is considered suitable only for the young, (2) because there are so many other substances, such as cleaning fluids and nail polish, that can be sniffed for the same effect and are more easily available, and (3) because manufacturers are replacing the toluene with harmless chemicals and sometimes adding foul smelling compounds to discourage sniffing.

GLUTETHIMIDE. A nonbarbiturate sedative/hypnotic that is sold under the trade name Doriden. It is used medically to induce sleep and as a sedative. When abused it results in euphoria and relaxation. If the dosage is too high, though, the individual reacts as to alcohol or barbiturate intoxication, including slurred speech, memory and concentration problems, physical impairment, and tremors. Abrupt withdrawal can be very serious, leading to anxiety attacks, seizures, cramps, chills, difficulty in swallowing, and numbness of the hands and feet. Up to 25 percent of addicts die if they undergo untreated withdrawal. Glutethimide is often used with codeine and called **HITS.** See **HITS.**

GOD'S MEDICINE. Slang for **MORPHINE.**

GOLD. Any gold-colored, potent marijuana, such as Acapulco Gold, Colombian Gold, or Kona Gold.

GOLD DUST. Slang for **COCAINE.**

GOLD LEAF. Same as **GOLD.**

GOODS. Slang for narcotics or any drugs.

GOOD STUFF. High quality heroin or other drug.

GOOF BALLS. Slang for **BARBITURATES.** The term comes from the goofy, silly, or stupid way barbiturate abusers behave.

GOOFER. A barbiturate user.

GOOFING. Acting in a drunken, uncoordinated way under the influence of a drug.

GORILLA PILLS. Slang for **BARBITURATES.**

GOW HEAD. A narcotics user.

GRAIN ALCOHOL. Alcohol made from the seed of grains, such as wheat, corn, rye, oats, rice, or millet.

GRASS. Slang for **MARIJUANA.**

GRASS BROWNIES. Brownies or cookies baked with marijuana.

GRAVY. A mixture of blood from an addict's arm and heroin in a syringe used for injecting the drug.

GREASY JUNKY. A narcotics addict who chooses to beg or run errands to get money for drugs.

GREEN. Any green-colored, low-potency marijuana, such as Mexican Green.

GREFA, GRETA, GREIFO, GRIFA, GRIFFO. Slang for **MARIJUANA.**

GROOVING. Enjoying drug-induced intoxication and euphoria.

GROUND CONTROL. A person who cares for someone using LSD; to help in case of a panic reaction.

GUM. A form of opium that can be eaten.

GUN. Slang for the hypodermic needle used to inject drugs.

GUNGA, GUNGEON, GUNJA, GUNJEH. Slang for **MARIJUANA.**

GUTTER. The vein (median cubital) on the inside of the elbow that is favored for injecting drugs.

H

H. Slang for **HEROIN.**

HABIT. A craving for and dependence on drugs.

HABIT-FORMING. Refers to any drug that may produce either physical or psychological dependence or both.

HABITUATION. A desire, rather than a compulsion, for a drug. Sometimes defined as being less intense than an addiction. The term has largely been replaced by "dependence."

HALF LOAD. Twelve to fifteen bags of heroin bought by the pusher from the wholesaler for sale on the street.

HALFWAY HOUSE. A facility that typically offers recovered addicts a place to live and some amount of treatment and counseling, while leaving them free to be away during the days and on weekends.

HALLUCINATION. The perception of sounds, visions, smells, or odors that do not exist in reality, but arise from the individual's own mind.

HALLUCINOGENS. Drugs that produce hallucinations, from the Latin, *hallucinari,* "to wander mentally," and the Greek, *genes,* "be born." They are mind-altering drugs that bring about changes in thought, self-awareness, emotion, and sensation. LSD, mescaline, and PCP are the best-known hallucinogens. These drugs are also called psychedelics, a word that Dr. Humphrey Osmond coined in 1956, meaning "revealing to the mind."

More than with any other drugs, reactions to hallucinogens depend on what the users expect to happen and with whom they take the drug. The first reaction, usually within a half hour, is euphoria that borders on ecstasy. The users feel bright and creative, although they may suffer wild changes of mood.

This stage is followed by a heightening of all experiences. Sounds are louder, colors brighter, smells stronger. There is also some confusion of the senses, with users reporting being able to hear the color green or see the smell of a flower. Floors and walls seem to sway, and time and space either stretch out far beyond normal or shrink.

And finally, there may be the hallucinations, with the unreal seeming to be real. Most of the hallucinations are visual, but the senses of hearing, touch, smell, and taste are also sometimes involved. In most cases, the hallucinations are strongly experienced for a short time, and the user then returns to normal. A few users experience what they call a "bad trip," and find the hallucinations frightening and horrifying. In a small percentage of cases, the hallucinations continue for an extended period or return, called a flashback, after a period of normalcy. In some people, these reactions resemble severe mental illnesses called psychoses. While most users do develop a tolerance for the hallucinogens, there is seldom a physical dependence. The psychological dependence is seldom strong enough to require daily use.

HALOPERIDOL. An antipsychotic tranquilizer sold under the trade name Haldol.

HAND-TO-HAND. Picking up the drugs from the dealer directly rather than having them left, or "dropped," somewhere to be collected by the buyer.

HARD DRUGS. A term not too clearly defined that usually refers to the more dangerous and addictive drugs, mostly narcotics, such as cocaine, crack, morphine, and opium.

HARRY. Slang for **HEROIN.**

HASH. Slang for **HASHISH.**

HASHISH. The drug produced from the tops and leaves of the female *Cannabis sativa* plant, which also produces marijuana. Hashish, though, is about eight times stronger than marijuana. The substance is usually sold in small, dark-brown rectangular lumps; the darker the color, the stronger the active ingredient, THC (tetrahydrocannabinol). It is usually smoked in a water pipe, or hookah, that cools the smoke and allows the user to control the intake of the drug. The name comes from Hasan-ibn-al-Sabbah, the eleventh-century Persian who founded the Assassins and gave his name both to hashish and assassins.

The effects of hashish are similar to those of mescaline; in higher quantities the effects resemble those of LSD. Many different reactions to hashish have been reported: distorted perception of the user's body, a split personality as though the individual is really two people, unreal feelings about space and time, intensification of all experiences, hallucinations, delusions of being all-powerful, and general feelings of anxiety, dread, and paranoia. When swallowed or smoked in larger amounts, it puts the user into a deep sleep.

There seems to be no tolerance of hashish, so the same dose is all that even long-time users require. This highly potent and concentrated hallucinogenic substance is clearly addicting.

HASH OIL. A highly-concentrated extract from the *Cannabis sativa* plant that is extremely potent, containing up to 60 percent THC (tetrahydrocannabinol). It is a thick liquid that can be anywhere from dark-brown to clear-yellow in color. Users put drops of hash oil on marijuana or tobacco cigarettes to increase their potency.

HAWK, THE. Slang for **LSD.**

HAY. Slang for **MARIJUANA.**

H-CAPS. Capsules of heroin, though now mostly replaced by envelopes of the drug.

HEAD. Someone who is a frequent, habitual drug user, although not necessarily a drug addict.

HEAD DRUGS. Drugs that affect the mind; mostly stimulant drugs.

HEAD SHOPS. Stores that sell drug paraphernalia.

HEARTS. Slang for **AMPHETAMINES.**

HEAVEN DUST. Slang for **COCAINE.**

HEAVENLY BLUE. The trade name of a variety of the morning glory plant whose seeds produce hallucinogenic effects.

HEAVY DRUGS. Those drugs, such as heroin, cocaine, and narcotics, that can produce a dependency.

HEMP. The fiber from the *Cannabis sativa* that is used to make rope.

HENRY. Slang for **HEROIN.**

HEPTABARBITAL. A short-acting barbiturate that acts as a sedative/hypnotic.

HER. Slang for **COCAINE.**

HERB. Slang for **MARIJUANA.**

HEROIN. A narcotic drug, diacetylmorphine hydrochloride, derived from morphine, that in turn is derived from the poppy plant, *Papaver somniferum.* First developed by the chemists of Bayer Company in Germany in 1898, it was immediately touted as a "heroine" drug, a more potent analgesic than morphine, a cough suppressant, and one that could cure opium or morphine addiction. Later the name was shortened to heroin.

Heroin is a white, odorless, crystalline powder that is soluble in water and has a bitter taste. Since it was believed to be nonaddictive, heroin soon found use as the active ingredient in a number of cough remedies and other patent medicines. By the time doctors had discovered that heroin was fully as addictive as morphine, heroin had spread worldwide throughout the entire drug culture.

Most of the heroin consumed in the United States comes from Turkey. Other major sources are Mexico; the so-called "Golden Triangle" area of Burma, Laos, and Thailand in Southeast Asia; and various countries in the Middle East.

While some heroin users sniff the powder, most inject it either under the skin ("skin popping"), into a vein ("mainlining"), or into a muscle ("muscling"). The users dissolve the powder in water, heat the solution in a spoon held over a flame, and then draw the liquid up in a hypodermic needle for the injection.

Since there is no easy way to measure the purity of heroin bought on the street, there is always the danger of an overdose. A mild overdose of heroin usually results in a stupor or a very heavy sleep. A larger overdose may lead to a coma, with a completely limp body, slow, shallow breathing, and cold, clammy skin. In the most severe cases of overdose, the person goes into convulsions, stops breathing, and dies.

Occasional use of heroin does not necessarily lead to addiction. But over a long period of time, users do develop a tolerance for the drug and both a psychological and physical dependency. Because of this compulsive craving, many heroin abusers are forced to spend all of their time getting their next "fix." This means robbing and stealing, selling the stolen goods, finding a heroin dealer with high-quality drugs, going to a place to inject the drug—and all the while watching out for the police.

Since narcotics have a sedative effect, most of the crimes committed by narcotics users are nonviolent. The only time they become violent is when they are desperate for a fix. Arrests of heroin addicts are common, and the jail sentences forcibly break the dependency. But on release, most users return to their habit, and the cycle starts all over again.

HEXOBARBITAL. A short-acting barbiturate, classified as a sedative/hypnotic.

HIGH. The pleasurable effects that accompany, or follow use of a drug.

HIM. Slang for **HEROIN.**

HIPPIE. Someone who follows a way of life that renounces material things and believes that it is possible to achieve deep insight into life through the use of drugs as well as introspection, alternate religious experiences, a sharing, nonmaterialistic style of life, and great freedom in sexual matters. The hippie movement peaked in cities like San Francisco and New York in the 1960s.

HIT. A drug dose that is injected, swallowed, or smoked. Also, the purchase of a drug.

HITS. Combination of glutethimide and codeine. Usually called "one on one" or "two on two", referring to the number of glutethimide pills and the number of codeine pills or the number on Tylenol with codeine, referring to the amount of codeine present.

HIT THE PIPE. To smoke opium.

HIT THE SEWER. To inject heroin into a vein.

HOG. The slang term for marijuana used by the American soldiers in Vietnam. Also, slang for **PCP**.

HOMEGROWN. Marijuana grown in or near one's home for personal use rather than for sale.

HOOKAH. A water pipe used for smoking tobacco, marijuana, or hashish in which the smoke is bubbled through water, cooling the smoke and making it less harsh.

HOOKED. Dependent on a drug, usually a narcotic.

HOP. Slang for **OPIUM.**

HOP HEAD. Someone addicted to heroin or opium or another narcotic.

HOPS. The dried flowers of the hop vine that are used to flavor beer.

HORN. To sniff a drug such as cocaine or heroine.

HORRORS. A panic reaction or any other bad reaction to a drug.

HORSE. Slang for **HEROIN.**

HOT SHOT. An injection of heroin that is fatal because it contains a poison, such as cyanide or strychnine.

HUBBLE-BUBBLE. Slang for **HOOKAH.**

HUFFER. Someone who sniffs a deliriant such as cleaning fluid or glue.

HUSTLER. Someone who is actively trying to raise money for a drug purchase, usually using criminal means.

HYDROCARBONS. A large group of compounds composed of carbon and hydrogen that evaporate quickly at room temperature. They act as depressants of the central nervous system and are often inhaled for their intoxicant effects. Among the better-known hydrocarbons are gasoline, naphtha, toluene, carbon tetrachloride, and benzene.

HYDROMORPHINE HYDROCHLORIDE. A narcotic analgesic that is five times stronger as a pain killer than morphine. Withdrawal symptoms are similar to those of morphine. Trade name—Dilaudid.

HYOSCYAMINE. The hallucination-causing drug found in such plants as jimsonweed, datura, henbane, and belladonna.

HYPE. A narcotics addict who uses a hypodermic needle. Also, a phony story or hoax.

HYPNOTICS. Drugs that induce sleep.

I

ICE. Slang for a smokeable form of methamphetamines.

ICE CREAM HABIT. Occasional, moderate use of drugs.

IDIOT PILLS. Barbiturates or other types of sedative pills.

IMIPRAMINE HYDROCHLORIDE. An antidepressant drug sold under the trade name Tofranil.

INDIAN HAY. Slang for **MARIJUANA.**

INDIAN HEMP. Slang for **MARIJUANA.**

INEBRIATED. In a drunken state, usually as a result of drinking alcohol.

INGESTION. Introducing a substance, such as a drug, into the body, usually by swallowing.

INHALANTS. Substances that give off fumes inhaled for their deliriant effects, such as cleaning fluid, nail polish, glue, etc.

INJECTION. A means of introducing a drug into body tissues using a hypodermic needle or a syringe. Drugs may be injected into a muscle, a vein, or beneath the skin.

INTO. To be deeply involved with something, such as drug use. ("He's *into* cocaine.")

INTOXICATION. A state in which an individual's normal functioning is seriously disturbed. It usually refers to the drunkenness from the effects of alcohol, which include slurred speech, unsteady gait, euphoria, increased activity, wild emotional swings, and, in the most severe cases, stupefaction.

INTRAMUSCULAR. Within the muscles, a frequent site of narcotic injections.

INTRAVENOUS. Within a blood vessel, a frequent site of narcotics injections.

IV. Short for **INTRAVENOUS.**

J

J. Slang for marijuana cigarette.

JAB. To inject a drug.

JAG. A state of intoxication, usually brought about by a drug.

JAM. Slang for either **COCAINE** or **AMPHETAMINE.**

JAMMED. Describing someone who has taken an overdose of drugs.

JANE. Slang for **MARIJUANA.**

JEFFERSON AIRPLANE. Originally a famous rock group. Now a device for holding the butt of a marijuana cigarette. It is made by splitting a used paper match in two, placing the butt between the halves, and holding it all together with the fingers.

JIMSON WEED. Common name for the plant, *Datura stramonium*. The drug made from the plant can cause hallucinations.

JINGO. Slang for **MARIJUANA.**

JOINT. A hand-rolled marijuana cigarette.

JONES. Either a drug habit or the symptoms that follow withdrawal from the drug.

JOY JUICE. Slang for **CHLORAL HYDRATE.**

JOY POP. To inject a narcotic, usually heroin, into muscles or under the skin.

JUNK. Slang for **HEROIN.**

JUNKIE. Someone addicted to heroin.

K

KEY. A kilogram (2.2 pounds) of a drug; often used to describe a block of marijuana of that weight.

KHAT. A central nervous system stimulant found in the leaves of the *Cathaedulis* plant. The usual method of ingestion is chewing the fresh leaves, which reduces fatigue and sleepiness, curbs hunger, and gives a general feeling of exhilaration.

KICK. Either the euphoric reaction to a drug or to break a drug habit.

KICKBACK. To return to drug use after stopping.

KIEF. Either the dried flower pods of the marijuana plant, a mixture of marijuana and tobacco, or a general word for marijuana. Also spelled kif or keef.

KILO. Short for kilogram (2.2 pounds). Heroin and marijuana are often prepared and shipped in kilogram packages.

KILTER. Slang for **MARIJUANA.**

KINDLING. The powerful effects of cumulative cocaine use on the body that may include shaking, stiffness, unconsciousness, or highly nervous behavior.

KING KONG. A very powerful heroin addiction or highly nervous behavior.

KING KONG PILLS. Slang for **BARBITURATES.**

KIT. Equipment for injecting drugs, usually including a hypodermic needle, eyedropper, cotton, bottle cap or spoon, water, and a strap to tie around the arm to help locate a vein for the injection.

KNOCKOUT DROPS. A mixture of chloral hydrate and alcohol that causes loss of consciousness.

L

L. Slang for **LSD.**

LAAM. Levo-alpha-acetylmethadol, a drug sometimes used in maintenance treatment programs. Currently, methadone is the more popular maintenance drug. Compared to methadone, LAAM needs to be taken only three times a week instead of daily, does not produce as quick a high, and seems to have a more level, sustained effect.

LADY SNOW. Slang for **COCAINE.**

LAME. Slang for someone who does not do drugs; a conventional person.

LAUDANUM. A solution of about 10 percent opium in alcohol. This was the first medicinal, non-prescription use of opium; it was used to treat a wide variety of illnesses and led to many cases of opium addiction.

LAUGHING GAS. The common name for the anesthetic gas, nitrous oxide.

LAY. To smoke opium or marijuana.

LAY DOWN. To smoke opium while lying down.

LAYOUT. Originally the equipment used for smoking opium but now broadened to include the equipment for injecting narcotics as well.

LBJ. Slang name for a hallucinogen, JB 336-N-Methyl-3 Piperdyl benzitate hydrochloride.

LEAPERS. Slang for **AMPHETAMINES.**

LEBANESE A brownish-red hashish that comes from Lebanon.

LEGAL HIGHS. A reference to the several herbs, spices, plants, and chemicals that are completely legal but that have psychoactive properties. Among the better-known such substances are nutmeg, catnip, dill, cinnamon, hydrangea leaves, niacin, green pepper, banana pulp, and parsley.

LEGALIZATION. Making legal a behavior that had formerly been considered illegal.

LEMON. Either a drug of very low potency or a counterfeit drug.

LETTUCE OPIUM. A wild lettuce plant, *Lactura virosa,* that produces mild effects somewhat similar to those of opium.

LEVALLORPHAN. A drug that reverses the effects of morphine and is used to treat overdose. Chemically, it is 1-3-hydroxy-N-allymorphinian tartrate.

LEVO-ALPHA-ACETYLMETHADOL. See **LAAM.**

LEVORPHANOL TARTRATE. A narcotic analgesic that is more potent than morphine. Prolonged use leads to addiction and severe withdrawal symptoms. Trade name—Levo-Dromoran.

LIBRIUM. Trade name for an antianxiety tranquilizer, chlordiazepoxide hydrochloride, that is widely used to treat nervousness and anxiety. In high doses it acts like a barbiturate, with such possible effects as intoxication, stimulation, loss of coordination, delirium, drowsiness, rage, and confusion. Excessive use over a prolonged period results in a physical dependency, and the abuser may suffer withdrawal symptoms—including mental upset, depression, loss of appetite, agitation, and insomnia. A number of people have committed suicide by taking a significant overdose of Librium. It is commonly used to treat withdrawal symptoms during detoxification from alcohol.

LID. A sale unit of marijuana, usually about one ounce, that contains enough of the drug to make about forty marijuana cigarettes.

LIDOCAINE. A local anesthetic.

LID POPPERS. Slang for **AMPHETAMINES.**

LIGHT STUFF. Drugs, such as marijuana, that some think do not cause addiction, as opposed to the "heavy drugs," such as heroin and cocaine, that are accepted as addictive.

LIGHT UP. To smoke marijuana.

LINE. The vein in the arm used to inject narcotics or a short narrow line of cocaine to be sniffed.

LITHIUM. An antipsychotic drug that is used to control the manic phase of manic depression.

LOAD. Twenty-five bags of heroin held together with a rubber band for delivery to a dealer.

LOADED. In a state of intoxication.

LOCO WEED. Slang for **MARIJUANA.** The term also refers to the wild plant, *Astrafulus mollisimus,* that causes intoxication in cattle.

LORFAN. Trade name for levallorphan tartrate, a synthetic drug that reverses the effects of narcotics. It does not diminish the analgesic effects of the narcotic but does lessen the danger of depression of the respiratory system.

LSD. A potent hallucinogenic drug, lysergic acid diethylamide-25, that produces intense psychoactive effects. LSD is 5,000 times more potent than mescaline and 200 times more potent than psilocybin. Just one ounce of LSD is enough to produce 300,000 individual doses!

LSD was first developed in Switzerland in 1938 by Dr. Albert Hoffman from the fungus ergot (*Claviceps purpurea*) that grows on the rye plant. Its psychoactive effects were discovered in 1943 when Dr. Hoffman accidentally ingested some of the drug. He reported feeling dizzy and trance-like and having weird fantasies and strange visions. Because the experience was pleasant, Dr. Hoffman tried some more LSD and had the same reactions. He realized that he was experiencing the same symptoms as those with mental disease and thought the drug might be a useful tool in researching mental illness.

For nearly twenty years scientists studied LSD, but made no significant discoveries. Then, in 1960, Dr. Timothy Leary, a psychologist at Harvard University, learned about the drug and started doing experiments on its uses and effects. He also started using it for recreational, nonscientific purposes, just enjoying its powerful, mind-altering effects, called "trips." Word soon spread on the remarkable "trips" Dr. Leary was experiencing with LSD, and recreational use of the drug was taken up by people, mostly young, throughout the world.

LSD is a colorless, odorless, tasteless liquid. For many years, LSD was taken by means of placing a drop on a sugar cube and swallowing it. Now it is more often in tablet form, in thin square of gelatin ("window panes"), or soaked into pieces of heavy paper ("blotter acid").

The effects of LSD start in about a half hour and last up to twelve hours, though there are many reports of a recurrence of the drug's effects up to eighteen months later—even without taking the drug. In addition to the mental changes, LSD may also cause trembling and shaking, rise in blood pressure, dry mouth, and dilated pupils. Sometimes, though, there is heightened anxiety, nausea, feelings of panic, and fear of suffocating. This reaction is called a bad trip. Bad trips are mostly experienced by those who fear the drug or who take it in circumstances that are not comfortable.

Recent research on animals suggests that LSD might cause genetic damage, leading to damage in the offspring of LSD users. Because of this, and because of the many people suffering from bad trips, LSD has faded from popularity.

LUDING OUT. Taking Quaaludes, a trade name for methaqualone.

LUMINAL. Trade name for phenobarbital, a slow-onset, long-acting sedative/hypnotic barbiturate. Death from overdose is a danger. It is so slow-acting that by the time its effects are seen, it is too late for medical intervention.

LYSERGIC ACID DIETHYLAMIDE. See **LSD.**

M

M. Morphine or marijuana.

MACE. A spice made from nutmeg that acts as a mild stimulant and produces light-headedness.

MACON. Slang for **MARIJUANA.**

MACONHA. Slang for **MARIJUANA.**

MAGIC MUSHROOM. Slang for **PSILOCYBIN.**

MAINLINING. The act of injecting a drug, usually heroin, into a vein in the arm.

MAINTENANCE THERAPY. A treatment program in which a person dependent on a drug, such as heroin, is legally supplied with that drug or a drug, such as methadone, that will prevent withdrawal symptoms so that the person can function in society.

MAJOR TRANQUILIZERS. Term used to describe a group of tranquilizer drugs that are now more often called antipsychotic tranquilizers.

MAJOUN. Slang for **MARIJUANA.**

MAKE. To recognize and identify someone, usually applied to drug dealers and plainclothes police officers.

MAKE A CROAKER FOR A READER. Convincing a doctor to write a prescription for a narcotic.

MAN, THE. Either a police officer or a drug dealer.

M AND C. A mixture of morphine and cocaine, usually with four parts morphine to one part cocaine.

MANICURE. To clean marijuana by removing the stems and seeds.

MANITA. The milk sugar used to dilute heroin.

MAO INHIBITORS. Monoamine oxidase inhibitors, a group of antidepressant drugs, chemically related to the amphetamines, that are used as mood elevators. There are five major trade names in use: Marplan, Niamid, Nardil, Parnate, and Eutonyl.

MARIHUANA. An alternate spelling of **MARIJUANA.**

MARIJUANA. A mildly-hallucinogenic drug made from the hemp plant, *Cannabis sativa.* Over 5,000 years ago in China, doctors recommended the plant as a treatment for gout, rheumatism, malaria, constipation, loss of appetite, melancholy, and as an aid in childbirth. Since then, it has been used medically throughout the world.

By the twentieth century, though, with the appearance of many new drugs, marijuana's use in medicine dropped very considerably. By 1941, marijuana was removed from the official list of substances American doctors could prescribe. Recent research into the possibility of using marijuana to treat glaucoma and some forms of cancer, though, has led to renewed medical interest in the drug.

Marijuana contains over 400 different chemicals. The most important psychoactive drug in marijuana is known as THC, short for delta-9-tetrahydrocannabinol. The amount of THC varies according to where the plant is grown and whether the leaves, stem, or flowering tops are used. The percentage of THC ranges from less than 0.5 percent to as high as 7 percent. The greater the THC content, the stronger and more potent the marijuana.

Most Americans smoke marijuana in the form of loosely-rolled cigarettes that are called either "joints" or "reefers." Sometimes the marijuana is smoked in a pipe. When a group of people smoke marijuana together, the cigarette or pipe is usually passed from person to person. Occasionally the marijuana is eaten by baking it into brownies. Once in the body, the THC remains in the system for up to a month.

A first-time user of marijuana does not usually get high. But continued use begins to bring about intoxicating effects—a pleasant dreamy feeling, increased confidence, and a lessening of fears and anxieties. But there are other effects as well. Some users become talkative and giggly, others become silent and withdrawn; some get only pleasure, others develop "pot panic," a frightening fear of going insane.

Long-time marijuana smokers begin to show signs of damage from the drug. They have a slower reaction time, lose some motor coordination, and find it hard to concentrate and learn anything new. Problems with memory and perception of time and space also occur. Heavy users sometimes appear to be very slow and dull and to be confused to the point of being unable to carry on a conversation. Some doctors believe that this might be a permanent condition.

Smoking marijuana also brings about some physical changes. The most obvious is a reddening of the eyes. It also can cause chest pains and a faster heart beat, a dryness of the mouth, and hunger.

Although marijuana does not seem to cause physical dependence, the drug does lead to psychological dependence, so that chronic users find it very hard to stop or even cut their use of the drug. When a long-time, heavy user stops, the most common withdrawal symptoms are insomnia, nausea, restlessness, and a loss of appetite.

MARY. Slang for **MORPHINE** or **MARIJUANA.**

MARY JANE. Slang for **MARIJUANA.**

MATCHBOX. About one-fifth of an ounce of marijuana, which is enough for between five and ten cigarettes.

MDA. Short for methylenedioxyamphetamine, a drug found in nutmeg, that is similar in make-up to amphetamines and mescaline. MDA intensifies emotions, increases the desire to communicate with others, and gives greater insights into one's inner feelings. An overdose can cause skin irritation, profuse sweating, and mental confusion. Death can result from an extreme overdose.

MDMA. A synthetic amphetamine that is closely related to MDA. Marketed as Ecstasy, a "designer" drug, the substance was made illegal in 1986. See **ECSTASY.**

MEAN GREEN. Slang for **PCP.**

MEET. Getting together with a dealer to buy some drugs.

MEPERDINE HYDROCHLORIDE. Short for ethyl-1-methyl-4 phenyl piperidine-4-carboxylate, a synthetic narcotic analgesic that is sold under the trade name of Demerol. Widely used in childbirth and to relieve severe pain, meperdine has become a popular choice of drug abusers in the medical profession who use it for its euphoric effects.

MEPROBAMATE. An antianxiety tranquilizer that is classified as a sedative/hypnotic. Chemically, it is 2-methyl-2-n-propyl- 1,3-propanediol dicarbamate. Sold under the trade names Miltown and Equanil, among many others, it is prescribed to treat tension, anxiety, and insomnia. Meprobamate can produce psychological dependence; long-term, heavy users may also experience physical dependence and suffer tremors, hallucinations, stomach upset, and insomnia upon stopping.

MESCALINE. The hallucinogenic drug (chemically–3,4,5-trimethoxyphenylethylamine) that is extracted from the head or button of the peyote cactus *(Lophophora williamsii)* or is prepared in the laboratory. First identified in 1886 by the German scientist, Louis Lewin, mescaline alters consciousness, distorts the senses, and can produce hallucinations. It is ingested either as a white powder that is dissolved in water or as a capsule. Some psychological dependence may develop, but there is no evidence of a physical dependency.

MESEROLE. A thick marijuana cigarette.

METHADONE. A synthetic narcotic analgesic, less potent than heroin or morphine, that is used in maintenance therapy. Chemically known as 4,4-diphenyl-6-dimethylamino-3-heptanone, it was first formulated by German scientists who gave it the trade name Dolophine after Adolf Hitler, the German dictator during the 1930s and 1940s.

Methadone has found widespread use in heroin maintenance therapy treatment for several reasons:

1. It prevents heroin withdrawal symptoms.

2. It satisfies the addict's need for a drug.

3. It blocks the effects of heroin.

4. Its effects are long-lasting, about twenty-four hours, which is much longer than the effects of heroin.

5. It can be taken orally, and does not need to be injected as heroin does.

6. It costs less than heroin and, since it is synthetic, is easily available.

The hope with methadone maintenance therapy is that the addict will be able gradually to break the heroin dependency and return to normal functioning. Critics, though, argue that methadone is also addictive and that it is almost as disruptive as a heroin habit. Some recommend LAAM as an alternative, since it does not require a daily dose.

METHAMPHETAMINE HYDROCHLORIDE. A stimulant of the central nervous system, it is the favored drug of habitual amphetamine users. They usually take it by intravenous injection, which produces the effects immediately. The trade names are Methedrine and Desoxyn.

METHAQUALONE. A nonbarbiturate sedative/hypnotic that produces sleep for about six to eight hours. Chemically known as 2-methyl-3-ortho-tolyl-4-quinzalonone, it was first developed in India in 1951 as a drug to treat malaria. When taken recreationally, it produces effects somewhat like mild drunkenness, including relaxation, contentment, release of inhibitions and passivity. Among the many trade names for methaqualone are Quaalude, Mandrax, Parest, Somnofac, and Sopor.

METHEDRINE. Trade name for **METHAMPHETAMINE HYDROCHLORIDE.**

METH FREAK. A heavy, habitual user of methamphetamine.

METHYLENEDIOXYMETHAMPHETAMINE. See **MDMA** and **ECSTASY.**

METHYLPHENIDATE HYDROCHLORIDE. A central nervous system stimulant that is manufactured under the trade name Ritalin. Mostly used to treat hyperactive children and overweight adults.

METHYPRYLON. A nonbarbiturate sedative/hypnotic. Prolonged usage can result in a physical dependence; sudden withdrawal can produce such severe symptoms as convulsions and delirium. Large doses can cause breathing difficulties and death. The trade name is Noludar.

MEXICAN BROWN. A brown-colored, high-potency marijuana from Mexico.

MEXICAN GREEN. The most common grade of marijuana coming from Mexico.

MEXICAN REDS. Seconal (sodium secobarbital) pills imported into the United States from Mexico.

MICKEY FINN. A drugged liquor named after a famous saloonkeeper in Chicago during the 1890s. It consists of the sedative/hypnotic chloral hydrate added to the alcoholic drink, which causes the drinker to lose consciousness.

MIKE. A microgram, which is one-millionth of a gram.

MILK SUGAR. Lactose, a powdery substance with a sweetish taste, that looks like heroin and is often added to heroin.

MILTOWN. Trade name for **MEPROBAMATE.**

MINOR TRANQUILIZER. A term used to describe a group of tranquilizer drugs that are now more often called antianxiety tranquilizers.

MJ. Slang for **MARIJUANA.**

MMDA. Short for 3-methoxyl-4,5-methylene dioxyphenyl isopropylamine, a drug found in nutmeg that intensifies feelings, both pleasant and unpleasant.

MOJO. A general slang word for drugs, especially cocaine.

MONKEY. A drug dependence so strong that it feels as though another is directing the user's actions.

MONKEY ON MY BACK. An addiction to narcotics. There are two possible derivations: One refers to a circus act in which a monkey holds on tightly to the back of another animal as it races around a track. The other goes back to the derogatory nickname, "monkey," used for a person of Chinese descent, and the expression, "Chinaman on my back," meaning an opium addiction because of the association that Chinese have with that drug.

MONOAMINE OXIDASE INHIBITORS. See **MAO INHIBITORS.**

MOOCAH. Slang for **MARIJUANA.**

MOOTA. Slang for **MARIJUANA.**

MORNING GLORY SEEDS. Seeds of the bindweed family of plants, *Convolvulaceae,* which have hallucinogenic effects. The seeds, which are either black or brown, can be chewed whole, can be ground into a powder and then eaten, or can have the psychoactive ingredient chemically removed and taken in that pure form.

MORPHINE. A very potent analgesic and the main active ingredient in opium. About 10 percent of natural opium by weight is morphine. First isolated in 1803 by the young German pharmacist, F. W. Sertutner, and named after Morpheus, the Greek god of dreams, morphine came to prominence during the Civil War in treating wounded soldiers. Its effects, in addition to the analgesia and general euphoria, include drowsiness, lessened mental and physical performance, reduced sex and hunger drives, changes in mood, mental clouding, difficulty in concentrating and learning, and apathy. Some of the side effects are constipation, nausea and vomiting, constriction of the pupils, yawning, heaviness of limbs, sweating, flushing, and a drop in body temperature.

Since heroin appeared on the scene in 1898, morphine use has been declining. The effect of the two drugs is almost identical and, since heroin is more potent, less of it is needed to achieve the same state.

MOTHER. Either a seller of drugs or marijuana.

MU. Slang for **MARIJUANA.**

MUGGLES. Marijuana cigarettes.

MUNCHIES. The very strong sensation of hunger that follows marijuana smoking.

MUSCLING. Injecting heroin into a muscle.

MUSHROOM. Slang for **PSILOCYBIN.**

MYRISTICIN. The hallucinogenic substance in nutmeg.

N

NA. See **NARCOTICS ANONYMOUS.**

NAIL POLISH, NAIL POLISH REMOVER. Quick-drying substances used to beautify the fingernails. Young people sometimes inhale the fumes of nail polish or nail polish remover to become intoxicated.

NALLINE. Trade name for nalorphine hydrochloride, a drug derived from morphine that has no analgesic effect but reverses the effects of morphine and other narcotics on the central nervous system. It also causes the pupils of someone taking narcotics to dilate or grow larger. If the person has not taken a narcotic, though, Nalline produces relaxation and drowsiness. In larger doses it may cause slurred speech, panic, anxiety, lethargy, hallucinations, and nausea.

NALLINE TEST. A test, often given to prisoners or parolees, to determine if they have been taking narcotics. The standard method for administering the Nalline test is first to measure the size of the subject's pupils before a constant source of light. Then three milligrams of Nalline are injected, and the pupil size is measured twenty, thirty, and forty minutes later. If the subject's pupil becomes more than 0.5 millimeters larger, it is considered evidence that there is a narcotic in the subject's body.

NALORPHINE. See **NALLINE.**

NALOXONE. A drug that reverses the effects of narcotics. Naloxone is widely used to treat overdoses of narcotics since it very effectively reverses depression of the respiratory system. It does not have any euphoric or analgesic effects, nor does it build up any dependence. If, however, a person is an abuser of narcotics, naloxone can cause withdrawal symptoms. Trade name—Narcan.

NALOXONE CHALLENGE. A test for the presence of narcotics in the system. It is the same as the Nalline test, except naloxone is used instead of Nalline.

NALTREXONE. A drug first developed in 1963 and very similar to naloxone. Naltrexone, however, offers the advantages that it can be taken orally, is long acting, produces few side effects, and does not produce withdrawal symptoms.

NAPHTHA. A solvent obtained by the distillation of petroleum that is inhaled for its intoxicating effected.

NARC. A drug enforcement officer; could be on the federal, state, or local level.

NARCAN. Trade name for **NALOXONE.**

NARCAN TEST. A test for the presence of narcotics in the system that works exactly like the Nalline test, except that the drug used is naloxone.

NARCOTIC. Any drug that blunts the senses, gives a feeling of well-being in small doses, and causes unconsciousness and even death in large doses. The word comes from the Greek, *narkotikos,* "numbing." Strictly defined, the main narcotics are heroin, opium, morphine, and methadone. In common usage, however, the term is often used to refer to all drugs, particularly those that can cause dependence.

NARCOTIC ANTAGONIST. A drug that blocks or reverses the effects of narcotics. Among the better-known narcotic antagonists are Nalline and naloxone.

NARCOTICS ANONYMOUS. A self-help group for recovered drug abusers. Patterned on Alcoholics Anonymous, NA was formed in 1953 and has some 700 chapters across the United States and many more around the world.

NATCH TRIPS. A high achieved with legal, natural substances, such as nutmeg, banana, cinnamon, mushrooms, morning-glory seeds, green peppers, wild rice, or peanut skins. These substances are usually either smoked or brewed in hot water. There is some question about whether the substances really do have psychoactive effects.

NATIVE AMERICAN CHURCH. A religion among Native Americans (American Indians) that combines Christianity, native religious rites, and the ritual use of peyote. The religion teaches brotherly love and high moral principles, forbids alcohol, and considers peyote a sacrament that brings God to the people. Members of the Native American Church believe that peyote can cure the sick as well as produce visions and altered consciousness that are part of their sacred observances.

NEBBIES. Slang for **NEMBUTAL.**

NEEDLE. The hypodermic needle used to inject drugs.

NEEDLE FREAK. Someone who injects drugs intravenously and enjoys the act of giving himself or herself the injection.

NEMBUTAL. Trade name for pentobarbital sodium, a short-acting barbiturate that acts as a sedative/hypnotic. A dependence can only be built up over a long period of very heavy use.

NEMISH. Slang for **NEMBUTAL.**

NEUROLEPTIC. Another word for **ANTIPSYCHOTIC TRAN-QUILIZER.**

NICKEL. Either a $5 packet of heroin or marijuana or a five-year prison sentence.

NICOTINE. The main active ingredient in tobacco; its chemical formula is $C_{10}H_{14}N_2$. Cigarettes contain between 0.5 and 2 milligrams of nicotine. It is held responsible for the addictiveness of smoking. It is one of the most addictive of all drugs.

Nicotine is probably the best-known ingredient of cigarette tar. The substance is a colorless, odorless oil compound with a particularly sharp taste. Taken alone, it is an extremely powerful poison; an injection of just a tiny drop, 70 milligrams of nicotine, can kill a human being.

Among the many general physical effects of nicotine are the irritation of lung tissue, the tightening of blood vessels, and the increase in blood pressure and heart rates. Nicotine is a central nervous system stimulant, yet in high doses it is a depressant. Even though regular smokers say it calms their nerves, they find it makes them dizzy. The Surgeon General's Reports of 1964 and 1982 came to a number of conclusions about smoking. Among them are the following: Cigarette smoking is a major cause of lung cancer; smoking is a contributing cause of heart disease, chronic bronchitis, and emphysema; and death rates are higher for smokers than for non-smokers. The 1988 Report pointed up the highly addictive effect of nicotine. Because of the many hazards of smoking tobacco, the Surgeon General's warnings now appear on every package of cigarettes.

NIMBY. Slang for **NEMBUTAL.**

NITROUS OXIDE. An analgesic and anesthetic that is commonly called laughing gas. It was discovered in 1776 by Joseph Priestly, who never inhaled it. In 1799, though, when Sir Humphrey Davy did breathe in the gas, he experienced both pleasurable exhilaration and uncontrolled giggling. Some years later, at a public exhibit of the joys of inhaling nitrous oxide, a young man who had been inhaling the gas, fell and badly gashed his leg—but felt no pain. Horace Wells, a dentist, saw what had happened and realized that the gas might have an important use in his dental office. Within a few years, nitrous oxide became widely accepted as an anesthetic, particularly for dental surgery.

While other drugs have replaced nitrous oxide as a dental analgesic and anesthetic, its recreational use has grown. When inhaled it makes the person giddy, giggly, and exhilarated, sometimes with hallucinations, for a period of about five minutes. Excessive use, though, can result in nausea, vomiting, loss of consciousness, or nerve damage in the arms and legs, usually because of a lack of oxygen.

NIXON. Narcotics of low potency.

NOCTEC. Trade name for **CHLORAL HYDRATE.**

NODDING. A dreamy, dozing state in which the individual's head is bowed and bobbing with the eyelids almost closed. This is the state narcotics users strive to achieve, and it usually follows a dose of the drug.

NOLUDAR 300. Trade name for **METHYPRYLON.**

NORML. Short for National Organization for the Reform of Marijuana Laws. Organized in 1970, NORML lobbies for the decriminalization of marijuana, destruction of criminal records for all marijuana-law offenders, recognition of the medical uses of marijuana, and more research on the effects of marijuana on women of childbearing age. They are, however, against drug abuse, the use of marijuana by children, and driving while under the influence of marijuana or any other drug.

NUMBER TWO SALE. The second conviction for selling narcotics, which carries much more severe penalties than the first conviction.

NUTMEG. The dried seeds of the East Indian evergreen tree, *Myristica fragrans.* In low doses it produces a brief, mild euphoria, along with lightheadedness, a sensation of floating, and stimulation of the central nervous system. High doses lead to rapid heartbeat, great thirst, anxiety, and sometimes a panic reaction. The seedcoat, called mace, has similar effects. Prisoners and sailors often use nutmeg as a substitute for other drugs.

O. Slang for **OPIUM.**

OD. See **OVERDOSE.**

OFF. Intoxicated by a drug.

OIL. The liquid extracted from hashish; it is very high in THC, the active ingredient of hashish.

ON. Using drugs or under the influence of a drug.

ONE AND ONE. Using both nostrils to inhale a drug.

ON THE NEEDLE. Injecting narcotics.

OPIATES. The drugs of the opium plant, *Papaver somniferum,* such as opium, morphine, and codeine, and the drugs derived from them, such as heroin and hydromorphone. They are classified as narcotic analgesics.

OPIOIDS. Synthetic drugs that are designed or manufactured to resemble the opiates. The term is usually extended to include the natural opiates found in opium (morphine and codeine), the opiates derived from opium (heroin and hydromorphone), and the completely synthetic drugs (meperidine and methadone).

OPIUM. A narcotic drug that is obtained by drying the milky discharge that comes from a cut in the unripe seedpod of the opium poppy (*Papaver somniferum*). Nearly 6,500 years ago, the ancient Egyptians knew that opium could kill pain. Then, when they found it also relieved anxiety, gave pleasure, and provided an escape from reality, they also used it for recreation. Since then, it has been used to treat some fifty different diseases. In seventeenth century England, it was called God's greatest gift to humanity because of its ability to relieve suffering.

Although the common expression is to say that someone "smokes" opium, it is not smoked in the same way a tobacco or marijuana cigarette is smoked. The usual method is to take a small bit of opium, called a pellet, and heat it, or "cook" it, over a flame. The opium is then placed in a pipe, and the "smoker" inhales the fumes.

In the second half of the nineteenth century, large numbers of illegal Chinese immigrants brought their opium habits with them to the United States. Opium dens, where people gathered to buy and smoke opium for pleasure, sprang up. Opium use and abuse spread throughout the country. By the early twentieth century, though, opium use was dropping. New and more effective analgesics were replacing its medical applications. And drug abusers found heroin to be a more powerful drug. Today, opium is mostly confined to medicinal use as paregoric (made of opium and camphor) and laudanum (opium and alcohol), which some addicts use when heroin is not available.

OPTIMIL. Trade name for **METHAQUALONE.**

ORGANIC DISORDER. A disease that is the result of a known change in body structure.

OUNCE MAN. A high-level distributor of heroin.

OUTFIT. The equipment for injecting drugs.

OVERCHARGED. Suffering from the effects, which range from sleepiness to a coma, that come from taking too large a dose of a drug, usually a narcotic.

OVERDOSE. Taking a quantity of a drug, usually an opiate or sedative, that is larger than what is normally or safely taken. An overdose, which usually depresses the central nervous system, may lead to coma and death.

OVERJOLT. Same as **OVERDOSE.**

OXAZEPAM. A minor tranquilizer manufactured under the trade name of Serax.

OXYCODONE HYDROCHLORIDE. An analgesic used to relieve moderate pain; it is derived from morphine. Prolonged use can result in dependence and withdrawal symptoms similar to that of morphine. Trade names—Percodan, Perocet-5, Tylox.

OXYMORPHONE HYDROCHLORIDE. A narcotic analgesic made from morphine that is a much more potent pain killer than morphine. Physical dependence follows long-term use, and ceasing use can cause withdrawal symptoms like those of morphine withdrawal. Trade name—Numorphan.

P

P. Slang for **PEYOTE** or **PCP.**

PACKED UP. Intoxicated by a drug.

PAD. Originally a place where drugs are taken, but now meaning the place where someone lives. The term comes from the pads on which opium smokers lie.

PANAMA GOLD. A potent marijuana from Panama that is gold in color.

PANAMA RED. A potent marijuana from Panama that is red in color. Also called **P.R.**

PANATELLA. Originally a very expensive cigar, but now a slang word for a big, thick, potent marijuana cigarette.

PANIC MAN. A drug addict who cannot obtain drugs.

PANIC REACTION. The most common bad reaction to a drug. The symptoms usually include overwhelming fear, anxiety, and an inability to move or make decisions. Most of the drug cases that come to the attention of psychiatrists are people who have had or are having a panic reaction. A panic reaction can be triggered by any drug and occasionally may come long after the last drug use.

PANTOPON. Trade name for a preparation of opium in its natural state but with all the inert material removed. It is manufactured as an analgesic to replace morphine.

PAPAVERINE. A natural part of opium that depresses the heart and relaxes blood vessels. Unlike morphine and codeine, other parts of opium, it has no analgesic or euphoric effects.

PAPER. Folded piece of paper that contains narcotics. Also a piece of heavy paper soaked with LSD.

PAPERS. The cigarette papers used to roll marijuana cigarettes.

PARACKIE. Slang for **PARALDEHYDE.**

PARALDEHYDE. A potent, fast-acting, nonbarbiturate sedative/hypnotic that was developed in 1829. Its original uses were to calm alcoholics with delirium tremens and psychotic patients, but because of its unpleasant odor and bitter taste it has largely been replaced by the barbiturates. The most frequent cases of addiction to paraldehyde occur among alcoholics who had been treated with the drug and developed a liking for it. Curiously enough, the withdrawal symptoms are similar to those of alcohol, including hallucinations, convulsions, and delirium tremens.

PARANOIA. A state of fear and suspicion that is much more extreme than is called for by the actual situation. Drug users show symptoms of paranoia because of the specific effects of certain substances—cocaine, LSD, PCP—on the brain.

PARAPHERNALIA. The equipment needed for drug use, which varies with the way the drug is taken. Users require different materials depending on whether the substances are smoked, injected, or snorted.

PAREGORIC. A mixture of about 4 percent opium in alcohol, along with camphor, anise oil, benzoic acid, and glycerin. It was first prepared in the early eighteenth century and has been used to control diarrhea and to relieve the pain of teething in babies. Paregoric is seldom used medically now, but addicts who cannot obtain heroin will drink up to a quart of paregoric a day to replace the heroin they crave. Also called **P.G.**

PAREST. Trade name for **METHAQUALONE.**

PARSLEY. Slang for **PCP.**

PARTYING. A social gathering where drugs are used.

PCP. Common name for phencyclidine, a depressant drug that acts as a powerful hallucinogen. Chemically it is 1-(1-phencyclohexyl) piperidine hydrochloride, and the trade name is Sernyl. First synthesized in 1959, PCP was originally used as an anesthetic, but because it caused confusion and delirium such use stopped. It is now used only as an anesthetic on animals. Since 1967, PCP has been a drug of abuse because it is easily available, cheap, and produces effects that fall between those of marijuana and LSD.

PCP is a white powder that dissolves in water. Most often it is scattered on leaves of parsley, marijuana, tobacco, oregano, or mint and then smoked. The effects are feelings of euphoria and relief from pain. Blurred vision, slurred speech, drowsiness, heavy sweating, and fast breathing often follow. PCP also seems to throw off inhibitions and to relieve feelings of agitation and anxiety. An obvious sign of PCP use is rapid, uncontrolled eye movement.

An overdose can cause mental confusion, hallucinations, and slurred speech. An even higher dose can produce the symptoms of severe mental disorder. A massive overdose may result in a coma and death. Many PCP deaths, though, are not the direct result of overdose, but come from accidents due to the mental confusion the drug produces.

PEACHES. Slang for **BENZEDRINE.**

PEARLS. Slang for **AMYL NITRATE.**

PELLETS. Slang for **LSD.**

PENTAZOCINE HYDROCHLORIDE. A potent narcotic analgesic that was first synthesized in 1961 and sold under the trade name Talwin. It was promoted as a nonaddictive painkiller as potent as morphine. Experience has shown, however, that users do develop a dependence and suffer such withdrawal symptoms as nausea, loss of appetite, insomnia, nervousness, depression, and anxiety. Even though some abusers choose pentazocine for the euphoria it produces, many are afraid of the drug for the hallucinations it creates.

PENTOBARBITAL SODIUM. See **NEMBUTAL.**

PENTOTHAL SODIUM. A very short-acting sedative/hypnotic. Medically it is used for short, minor surgery and before administering a general anesthetic for major surgery. In small amounts the drug lowers inhibitions and allows the user to speak freely of repressed throught and memories, which is why it is sometimes used by the police as a "truth drug." The drug also seems to make the user open to suggestions and more willing to accept thoughts and ideas presented by others.

PEP PILLS. Slang for **AMPHETAMINES.**

PER. Slang for prescription.

PERCOBARB. A combination of a morphine-related drug and a barbiturate that is used as an analgesic sedative/hypnotic. The manufacturer recommends percobarb for mild pain that causes sleeplessness, such as headache, arthritis, etc. Excessive, prolonged use can result in dependence and withdrawal symptoms similar to those of morphine withdrawal.

PERCODAN. A morphine-related drug used as an analgesic. Similar to Percobarb, but without the barbiturate.

PETER. Slang for **CHLORAL HYDRATE.** Also a general term for narcotics.

PETHIDINE. General term for **MEPERIDINE HYDROCHLORIDE.**

PEYOTE. A small, gray-brown cactus plant, *Lophophora williamsii,* with little heads or buttons that barely protrude from the ground. Native to northern Mexico and Texas, the plant contains the hallucinogen, mescaline. The mind-altering qualities of peyote have long been known to the Indians or Native Americans of that area, who use it in their religious services. They cut off the buttons of the plants and dry them in the sun. Then they either soak them in water and drink the liquid or eat them directly. The results are hallucinations that include intensified sensations, visual distortions, increased hearing ability, great clarity of thought, and the feeling of oneness with God. Along with these reactions, though, sometimes come chills, vomiting, and frightening terror and anxiety. Peyote does not seem to be addictive.

P.G. Slang for **PAREGORIC.**

PHENAZOCINE. A narcotic analgesic that is slightly more potent than morphine. Prolonged use can lead to withdrawal symptoms between those of methadone and morphine.

PHENCYCLIDINE. See **PCP.**

PHENOBARBITAL. A barbiturate sedative/hypnotic that is slow to start its action, but whose effects last for a long time. First used medically in 1912, it is prescribed to treat the convulsions of epilepsy and delirium tremens. Trade name—Luminal.

PHYSICAL DEPENDENCE. A change in the body after long or excessive use of a drug so that the person suffers very real withdrawal symptoms when the drug use is stopped. These symptoms, however, do not appear as long as the person continues taking the drug.

PICK UP. To smoke marijuana.

PIECE. A quantity of a drug, though the exact amount is not specified.

PILL. Originally a pellet of opium, but now meaning a barbiturate or amphetamine.

PILL HEAD. Someone addicted to barbiturates or amphetamines.

PIN. A marijuana cigarette that is rolled very thin.

PIN HEAD. Either a thin marijuana cigarette or a narcotics addict who uses an eyedropper and pin instead of a hypodermic needle.

PINKS. Slang for **SECONAL.**

PINNED. Narrowed eye pupils that can be caused by either heroin or morphine.

PIPE. A large vein.

PIT. The main vein going to the heart; considered the best vein for injecting narcotics.

POISON. Slang for either **HEROIN** or **COCAINE.**

POKE. A puff of smoke from a marijuana cigarette.

POP. Either to inject a drug or to swallow a drug in pill form.

POPPED. To be picked up or arrested by the police.

POPPERS. Small vials of amyl nitrite. To use the drug, the vial is broken in a handkerchief and then inhaled.

POPPY. Slang for **OPIUM.**

POT. Slang for **MARIJUANA.**

POTENCY. The relative strength of a drug. The more potent a drug, the more powerful it is and the less that is required to achieve a certain effect.

POTENTIATE. To increase the activity of a drug, usually by taking it along with a second drug. Alcohol, for example, potentiates the effects of many drugs, while depressant drugs potentiate one another.

POT PANIC. A bad reaction to marijuana.

P.R. See **PANAMA RED.**

PRELUDIN. Trade name for phenmetrazine hydrochloride, a central nervous system stimulant that works like amphetamine. It is used by those who want to lose weight as a diet depressant, but it also is a general stimulant and produces a feeling of euphoria.

Tolerance and dependence follow excessive use. Withdrawal symptoms include severe depression and fatigue.

PRINADOL. A narcotic analgesic recommended for very strong, long-lasting pain. It does produce physical dependence.

PROLIXIN. Trade name for flupenazine hydrochloride, an antipsychotic tranquilizer, used to control severe agitation and mental disorders in highly disturbed patients.

PROOF. A measure of the percent of alcohol in liquor. The proof number is twice the percentage of alcohol present. For example, a whiskey of 90 proof is 45 percent alcohol.

PSILOCYBIN. A hallucinogenic drug found in a number of mushroom plants, such as *Psilocybe mexicana.* The mushrooms have a bitter taste and acrid odor. When eaten, they cause muscle relaxation and mood changes, usually with bouts of wild laughter. This is followed by brilliant visions and sounds that may last up to five hours, after which there is a complete let-down with both physical and mental depression.

PSYCHEDELIC. A word coined in 1956 by Humphrey Osmond from the Greek *psyche,* "soul," and *delos,* "visible." It refers to the mind-altering, consciousness-expanding effects and visions of the hallucinogenic drugs, such as LSD, mescaline, and psilocybin.

PSYCHOACTIVE. Any drug that affects the central nervous system and alters a person's mood, perception, or consciousness.

PSYCHOLOGICAL DEPENDENCE. A strong craving for the pleasurable effects of a drug, such as euphoria, stimulation, hallucinations, sedation, exhilaration, and so on. Although stopping the drug after psychological dependence is established does not cause a specific physical reaction, it often leaves the former user depressed and uncomfortable and very eager to take the drug again.

PSYCHOTOGENIC. A drug or other factor that produces hallucinations and psychotic behavior.

PSYCHOTOMIMETIC. The ability of some drugs to produce behavior and feelings similar to those of a psychosis.

PSYCHOTROPIC. A reference to drugs that affect the mind; more specifically, drugs that are used in treating mental conditions.

PUFF. To smoke opium.

PURE. Slang for heroin that is not too heavily adulterated.

PURPLE HEARTS. Slang for **PHENOBARBITAL.**

PUSHER. A dealer in drugs who sells directly to the drug users.

PUT IT IN WRITING. Ways to smuggle drugs into prison or a drug treatment center, such as splitting open a post card and hiding the drug inside the two sheets or soaking a letter in a solution of a drug.

Q

QUAALUDE. See **METHAQUALONE.**

QUARTER BAG. A one-ounce bag of marijuana, worth about $25.

QUILL. A folded matchbook cover on which a powdered drug, usually cocaine, is placed and then snorted.

R

RACEHORSE CHARLIE. A user of narcotics.

RAGWEED. Low-quality marijuana.

RAINBOW. Slang for **TUINAL.**

RAINY DAY WOMAN. Slang for **MARIJUANA.**

RAP. To talk, especially using the vocabulary of those in the drug culture.

READER. A prescription for narcotics, usually obtained illegally.

RED. Slang for **PANAMA RED.**

RED AND BLUES. Slang for **TUINAL.**

RED BIRDS. Slang for **SECONAL.**

RED CHICKEN. Slang for **HEROIN.**

RED DEVILS. Slang for **SECONAL.**

RED DIRT MARIJUANA. Marijuana growing wild and uncultivated.

RED ROCK. Slang for heroin in granular form.

REDS. Slang for **SECONAL.**

REEFER. Slang for marijuana cigarettes.

REPLACEMENT DRUG. A drug that is prescribed to take the place of the one the patient has been abusing. Methadone is a common replacement drug for heroin.

RESERPINE. A drug found in the snakeroot plant, *Rauwolfia serpentina.* Used in a number of preparations as a tranquilizer, reserpine calms agitated or nervous patients, yet does not interfere with motor control. Reserpine is seldom used as a drug of abuse.

RIFLE RANGE. The ward of a hospital or drug treatment center for patients undergoing drug withdrawal.

RIG. Equipment for injecting drugs.

RIGHTEOUS. Either a high-quality drug or a person who can be trusted.

RIGHTEOUS BUSH. Slang for **MARIJUANA.**

RIPPED. Either very high on drugs or exhausted after drug use.

RIPPERS. Slang for **AMPHETAMINES.**

RITALIN. Trade name for methylphenidate hydrochloride, a stimulant of the central nervous system. Its effects are like those of the amphetamines, and it is used to treat mild depression and hyperactive children. Overdosage can result in hallucinations, delirium, convulsions, and coma. Like the amphetamines, Ritalin is addicting; abnormal movements or tremors and severe dependency can result from prolonged use. The abuser goes through withdrawal symptoms on stopping the drug.

ROACH. The butt end of a marijuana cigarette. In order not to waste any of the drug, the cigarette is smoked until it is very short and then held with some sort of device to avoid burning the fingers. When it is impossible to hold any longer, the cigarette is torn open and the unburnt marijuana saved for future use.

ROACH CLIP. Any device used to hold the short butt of a marijuana cigarette.

ROCKS. Pieces of cocaine in the form of crack or of heroin.

ROLL. A package holding a number of pills.

ROOT. Slang for a marijuana cigarette.

ROPE. Slang for **MARIJUANA.**

ROSES. Slang for **BENZEDRINE.**

RUN. A period of continuous heavy drug use. The term is especially applied to injections of amphetamine that go on for up to five days before the person collapses into a heavy sleep.

RUNNERS. People involved in drug-dealing who bring drugs to the United States from South America, Asia, and the Middle East.

Runners include pilots who fly shipments of drugs in, and small boat owners who use their craft to land drug shipments at isolated spots on the coasts.

RUSH. The first feelings of euphoria and well-being that come immediately after a drug injection. It is different from a high, which is the pleasurable feelings that continue over a longer period of time. Although the term was first used to refer to the reactions to heroin and the amphetamines, it now applies to several drugs.

S

SACRAMENT. Slang for **LSD**.

SACRED MUSHROOM. See **PSILOCYBIN.**

SALT SHOT. An injection of a saltwater solution given to someone who has just overdosed on heroin in the belief that it might revive the victim. Doctors do not find that it is of any help.

SAM. Slang for a federal narcotics agent, derived from Uncle Sam.

SAN PEDRO CACTUS. A tall, branching cactus that contains mescaline and has hallucinogenic effects.

SATCH. Cloth or paper saturated with a drug so that it will not be detected by narcotics officers.

SCAG. Slang for **HEROIN.**

SCARS. Marks left on the skin after injecting drugs; black and blue spots.

SCAT. Slang for **HEROIN.**

SCENE. A place where drugs are taken or the social arrangement for drug-taking in a particular area.

SCHMACK. Slang for **HEROIN.**

SCHMECK. Slang for **HEROIN.**

SCHOOLBOY. Slang for **CODEINE.**

SCOFF. To eat a drug.

SCOOP. As a noun, it is the folded matchbook cover used to snort cocaine; as a verb, it is the act of snorting cocaine through a folded matchbook cover.

SCOPOLAMINE. A nonbarbiturate sedative/hypnotic and muscle relaxant. It is the active ingredient found in henbane (*Hyoscyamus niger*) and several other plants. Some years ago it was found that scopolamine made people more willing to answer questions, and it was, therefore, used as a "truth drug." Currently it is used as a sedative to relax patients before surgery and in such nonprescription sleep preparations as Sominex, Sleep-eze, and Compose. Although large doses of scopolamine can produce euphoria and exhilaration, the drug can also produce very frightening hallucinations and is therefore not very often abused.

SCORE. To buy a drug.

SCRIPT. A prescription for narcotics.

SECONAL. Trade name for secobarbital, a fast-working, long-lasting barbiturate sedative/hypnotic. An overdose can result in depression of the central nervous system and respiration and lowered body temperature. A massive overdose leads to coma and death. Users develop a strong dependence after heavy, long-term use and suffer severe withdrawal symptoms on abruptly stopping.

SEDATIVES. A group of drugs that bring about calmness and relaxation and help to relieve tensions and anxieties.

SEGGY. Slang for **SECONAL.**

SERAX. A drug used to treat mild anxiety, nervousness, and tension. Prolonged use can lead to dependence, and some people suffer withdrawal symptoms after a relatively brief period of use.

SERNYL. Trade name for **PCP.**

SET. The physical and mental state of a person taking a drug, which may influence the reactions to the drug.

SETTING. The place, the other people present, and the surroundings where a drug is taken. A pleasant, friendly, attractive setting helps to make the drug-taking a positive experience.

SEWER. Vein into which narcotics are injected.

SHERMANS. Slang for **PCP.**

SHOOTING GALLERY. Place where narcotics addicts regularly gather to inject themselves or each other.

SHOOTING GRAVY. Injecting blood that has been drawn into the needle while injecting a narcotic. If the blood in the needle has coagulated, it is heated with water and the narcotic and is then injected.

SHOOT UP. To inject heroin or another narcotic.

SHORT COUNT. A smaller amount of a drug than specified.

SHORT PIECE. Either a very diluted drug or less of the drug than was paid for.

SHOVE. To sell drugs on the street level, related to someone pushing drugs.

SHYING. Heating opium in preparation for smoking.

SICK. Suffering the effects of withdrawal.

SIDE EFFECTS. All effects of a drug, except the specific effects for which the drug was taken.

SINSEMILLA. Very potent marijuana made from the flowering top of the unpollinated, seedless, female marijuana plant. The word comes from the Spanish *sin,* "without," and *semilla,* "seed." Sinsemilla has up to 6 percent THC, the psychoactive ingredient, while ordinary marijuana may only contain 1 percent THC. To grow sinsemilla, all male plants must be weeded out from the field to prevent pollination.

SIZZLE. Any narcotics that one is carrying.

SKID BAG. A container with heroin, usually in a dilute form.

SKIN. Paper for rolling marijuana cigarettes.

SKIN POPPING. Injecting a narcotic under the skin (subcutaneously). Drugs injected this way do not act as fast as those injected into a vein.

SKY ROCKETS. Slang for **AMPHETAMINES.**

SLEEPERS. Slang for **BARBITURATES.**

SLEEPWALKER. Someone taking heroin.

SMACK. Slang for **HEROIN.**

SMASHED. Intoxicated on drugs.

SMOKE. Slang for **HEROIN.**

SNAPPERS. Glass vials containing amyl nitrate.

SNIFFING. Inhaling the fumes of such substances as glue, nail polish, cleaning fluid, and so on.

SNOP. Slang for **MARIJUANA.**

SNORTING. Slang for sniffing a drug such as cocaine or heroin.

SNOW. Slang for **COCAINE,** from the white, flaky appearance of the substance.

SOAPERS. Slang for **METHAQUALONE.**

SOFT DRUGS. All drugs except narcotics. Some definitions, though, include all nonaddicting drugs as soft drugs.

SOFTBALLS. Slang for **BARBITURATES.**

SOLVENTS. Substances that can dissolve other substances and that evaporate easily. Among the more common solvents are glue, gasoline, nail polish, nail polish remover, cleaning fluids, and paint thinner. When the fumes from these solvents are inhaled they produce a short period of stimulation and euphoria followed by a lengthy, dream-like state. In addition, though, they depress the central nervous system, lower the heart and breathing rate, interfere with thought processes, and diminish muscle coordination.

SOMINEX. Trade name for **SCOPOLAMINE.**

SOMNAFAC. Trade name for **METHAQUALONE.**

SOMNOS. Trade name for **CHLORAL HYDRATE.**

SOPOR. Trade name for **METHAQUALONE**

SOPORIFIC. Inducing sleep.

SOURCE. A supplier of drugs, usually on the wholesale level.

SPACE BASE. A very potent mixture of crack and PCP that can easily produce hallucinations, violent behavior, and seizures.

SPACE CADET. Someone who is always in a state of drug intoxication.

SPACED OUT. In a state of altered consciousness as the result of drug use.

SPARKLE PLENTIES. Slang for **AMPHETAMINES.** The term derives from Sparkle Plenty, a character in the comic strip "Dick Tracy."

SPEED. A general reference to amphetamines, especially Methedrine.

SPEEDBALL. An injected mixture of heroin and cocaine. The cocaine makes the initial rush even more pleasurable, while the heroin controls and extends the high. Also, mixtures of heroin and amphetamine, Percodan and methamphetamine, and Dilaudid and cocaine.

SPEED FREAK. A chronic user of amphetamines.

SPIKE. A hypodermic needle.

SPLASH. The noun means amphetamines; the verb means to inject a drug.

SPLIT. To leave or run away from a place or situation.

SPOON. A spoon, with the handle bent into a loop so that a finger can pass through for steady holding, that is used to heat a mixture of heroin and water in preparation for injecting the drug. The term is also a measure of about one sixteenth of an ounce of pure heroin, which is sold to the dealer who adds materials that dilute the drug, before selling it on the street.

SPRING. To offer someone a marijuana cigarette at no cost.

SQUARE. Someone who does not do drugs and accepts all of the rules of society.

STAR DUST. Slang for **COCAINE.**

STAR SPEED. Same as **SPACE BASE.**

STASH. A place to hide drugs and the equipment to use the drugs.

STEAMBOAT. An empty toilet-paper roll that is used to get all the smoke from a marijuana cigarette butt. The butt is stuck through a hole in the side of the roll, and the smoker covers the far end of the roll with a hand and inhales the mixture of smoke and air. It was so named because the device resembles the smoke stack of a steamboat.

STEROIDS. A large group of organic compounds that includes various hormones. Anabolic steroids are derived from the male hormone, testosterone, and produce certain body changes in athletes who use them while training. The drugs help the body build muscle mass. They enhance performance and increase aggression and the drive to train harder. Some serious side effects include liver damage, high blood pressure, and addiction. The substances are banned in athletic competitions, such as the Olympics, and users are disqualified.

STICK. A marijuana cigarette.

STIMULANTS. Drugs that cause increased brain activity. They produce an elevation of mood, or euphoria, wakefulness and alertness, increased mental activity, more energy and less appetite. Along with this comes a speed-up in the heart rate and perspiration.

STING. To rob or to cheat.

STINKWEED. Slang for **DATURA.**

STONED. In a state of drug-induced intoxication—euphoric and elated.

STP. Common name for dimethoxymethamphetamine, which is called DOM by the company that manufactures it. STP is an extremely potent, long-lasting hallucinogen that is chemically related to amphetamines. The name comes either from the motor oil additive, which is advertised to provide more power, or is an acronym for **S**erenity, **T**ranquility, **P**eace.

STRAIGHT. Either someone who does not do drugs or someone not currently under the influence of a drug.

STRAW. Slang for **MARIJUANA.**

STREET ADDICTS. Persons who see themselves as addicts and behave in a way that fits into the drug culture. They are usually poor, often addicted to cheap wine ("winos"), live in the slums of a big city, and belong to a minority. The most admired of the street addicts are those who are "cool" and cunning.

STRUNG OUT. Weak, thin, and sick-looking because of a long-time addiction. Also, unable to obtain enough drugs to avoid withdrawal symptoms.

STUFF. Any drugs.

STUMBLERS. Slang for **BARBITURATES.**

STUPOR. A state of semiconsciousness in which the individual is not aware of the surroundings. Many drug users fall into a stupor as the result of a drug overdose.

SUBCUTANEOUS. Beneath the skin; one of the ways of injecting drugs.

SUGAR WEED. Marijuana soaked in sugar water to make it weigh more and to make it stick together in a block.

SWEAT IT OUT. To break a drug habit.

SWEET LUCY. Marijuana that has been soaked in wine.

SWING MAN. A seller of drugs.

SYNTHETIC. Made by a chemical process rather than found in nature.

T

T AND B. A drug that combines Talwin (pentazocine) and Pysibenzamine (tripelennamine). The initials come from Talwin and the blue color of the Pysibenzamine. Pentazocine is an analgesic, and Pysibenzamine is an antihistamine. When heated together and injected they produce an immediate euphoria that users compare to the "rush" of high-quality heroin. Although T and B poses serious health risks, including damage to the lungs, eyes, and brain, seizures, and convulsions, it is frequently abused because it is much cheaper than heroin and the user can be sure of its purity and potency.

TABS. Capsules containing LSD; any drug in tablet form.

TAKE OFF. To steal either money or drugs.

TAKE-OFF ARTISTS. Addicts who support themselves and their habit by robbing other addicts or dealers.

TAKING CARE OF BUSINESS. The daily activities of drug addicts that are necessary to obtain drugs. Many addicts look on "taking care of business" as a highly challenging, adventurous, and ultimately very rewarding style of life.

TALK DOWN. A method of treating someone undergoing a panic reaction or a bad trip as the result of drug use. The person doing the talking must be quiet, relaxed, and sympathetic and must explain, over and over again, that the present condition is due to the drug and is only temporary. It is also helpful to identify objects in the surroundings and to speak of people and places familiar to the drug user.

TALWIN. Trade name for **PENTAZOCINE HYDROCHLORIDE.**

TAPPING THE BAG. A way that dealers cheat, by removing a tiny bit of heroin from each bag they sell.

TAR. Crude opium.

TASTE. A small quantity of a drug that is given free before a purchase is made.

TEA. Slang for **MARIJUANA.**

TEA BAG. A marijuana cigarette.

TEN-CENT PISTOL. A bag that is offered as heroin, but that really contains poison.

TENS. Amphetamines in ten-milligram tablets.

TETRAHYDROCANNABINOL. The main psychoactive ingredient in marijuana. Often called by its initials, THC.

TEXAS TEA. Slang for **MARIJUANA.**

THAI STICKS. Very potent, seedless marijuana that is grown in Thailand. The tops of the marijuana plants are wound around sticks of bamboo and then tied together into bundles. Thai sticks are very expensive.

THIOPENTAL SODIUM. A sedative/hypnotic barbiturate that is extremely short-acting. Trade name—Pentothal.

THIRD EYE. The imaginary inward-looking eye that provides visions to those on hallucinogenic drugs, such as LSD.

THORAZINE. Trade name for chlorpromazine hydrochloride, an antipsychotic tranquilizer. Used to treat patients with schizophrenic and manic-depressive illnesses. Although there is no evidence of true physical dependence, there are some symptoms, such as nausea, vomiting, dizziness, and tremors on suddenly stopping.

THRUSTERS. Slang for **AMPHETAMINES.**

THUMB. A fat marijuana cigarette.

TICKET. A heavy paper or blotter containing LSD.

TIE. A cord, strap, belt, or necktie used as a tourniquet to raise a vein for a narcotics injection.

TIGHTEN UP. To take a drug, usually to smoke marijuana.

TIN. Marijuana packed in a can, such as a tobacco can.

TINGLE. The first effects of heroin, which are felt in the chest.

TLITILTZEN. The Aztec word for the black morning glory seeds, which are hallucinogenic.

TMA. Common name of 3,4,5-trimethoxphenyl-B-animopropane, a hallucinogen with stimulant properties that is stronger than mescaline but weaker than LSD.

TOAK. To smoke a marijuana cigarette. Also spelled toke.

TOBACCO. Dried leaves of the plant, *Nicotiana tabacum.* The main active ingredient in tobacco is nicotine, which has the ability to either stimulate or calm, depending on the state of the smoker.

Tobacco, though, has a number of harmful effects on the heart and lungs as well as being a proven cause of cancer.

TOFRANIL. An antidepressant rarely used for nonmedical purposes.

TOKE. See **TOAK.**

TOLERANCE. The build-up of resistance to the effects of a drug that occurs with continued use of the drug. Tolerance requires more of a drug dose to get the same effects as the original dose.

TOLUENE. Common name for methyl benzene, the main active ingredient in glue and paint thinner that causes mind-altering effects when sniffed.

TOOIES. Slang word either for Tuinal capsules or for barbiturates in general.

TOOLS. Equipment used for injecting drugs.

TOOT. A small sample of a drug given to someone considering making a purchase. Also a slang name for **COCAINE.**

TOP. A brand of cigarette paper used for rolling marijuana cigarettes. The word is pot, (slang for marijuana), spelled backwards.

TOPI. Slang for **PEYOTE.**

TORCH. Marijuana cigarette.

TORN UP. Intoxicated by a drug.

TORPEDO. An alcoholic drink containing chloral hydrate that causes unconsciousness. Also, a thick marijuana cigarette.

TOSSED. Searched for drugs.

TOXIC. Poisonous.

TOY. A small container for opium.

TRACKS. Both the scars on the skin and the collapsed vein that result from frequent heroin injections. Addicts often will wear clothes with long sleeves or have tattoos to cover their tracks.

TRAFFICKING. Dealing with the sale and shipment of drugs in large amounts, often across borders.

TRANQUILIZERS. A large group of drugs that depress the central nervous system. They relieve anxiety, agitation, and tension and sometimes relax the muscles. The tranquilizers also have some dangerous side effects, such as leading to addiction, potentiating the effects of other depressants, and, when overdosed, leading to coma and death. See also **ANTIANXIETY TRANQUILIZERS** and **ANTIPSYCHOTIC TRANQUILIZERS.**

TRANXENE. A commonly prescribed drug for mild anxiety, nervousness, and tension.

TRAVEL AGENT. Slang for **LSD.**

TREMORS. A shaking or trembling that is sometimes caused by an overdose of a drug or by sudden withdrawal from a drug.

TRIP. The experience that results from taking a hallucinogenic drug.

TRIP GRASS. Marijuana with amphetamine added.

TRIPPER. Someone who abuses hallucinogenic drugs.

TRIPS. Slang for **LSD**.

TUINAL. Trade name for a barbiturate that contains equal amounts of amobarbital sodium and secobarbital sodium. It is a short-to intermediate-acting sedative/hypnotic.

TURN ON. To introduce someone to drug use or to become intoxicated from drug use.

TURN ON, TUNE IN, DROP OUT. A 1960s slogan of the hippies and so-called flower children. The phrase means to take drugs, extend one's consciousness, and turn away from the materialistic world.

TWENTY-FIVE. Slang for **LSD**.

TWIST. A marijuana cigarette. The name comes from the way the ends of the cigarettes are twisted so that none of the drug falls out.

TWISTED. Suffering the symptoms and distress of withdrawal.

TYING UP. Wrapping a cord, strap, belt, or necktie tightly around the upper arm to make a vein stand out for a drug injection.

U

UNCLE. A federal narcotics agent. The name comes from Uncle Sam.

UP. In an intoxicated, exhilarated state.

UP AND DOWN THE LINES. Collapsed veins all over the arms.

UPPERS. Slang for **AMPHETAMINES.**

UPPIES. Slang for **AMPHETAMINES.**

UPS. Slang for **AMPHETAMINES.**

UPTIGHT. Tense, worried, nervous.

USING. Taking drugs, especially narcotics.

V

VALIUM. Trade name for diazepam, an antianxiety tranquilizer and muscle relaxant. The most prescribed drug in the United States, Valium can produce a dependence and withdrawal symptoms that include convulsions, tremor, cramps, and sweating. Overdose results in a condition like severe alcohol intoxication.

VERONAL. See **BARBITAL.**

VIPER. Long-time, habitual marijuana user.

VONCE. Butt of a marijuana cigarette.

VOYAGER. Someone on a hallucinogenic trip, especially one caused by LSD.

W

WACK. To increase the weight of a drug by adding impure or worthless material.

WACKY WEED. Slang for **MARIJUANA.**

WAKE UP. The first injection of the day for a narcotics addict.

WALLBANGERS. Slang for **METHAQUALONE.**

WASTE. To kill, destroy, or use up.

WASTED. Passed out from drug intoxication.

WATER. Slang for **AMPHETAMINES.**

WEDDING BELLS. Slang for morning glory seeds.

WEED. Slang for **MARIJUANA,** usually a low-potency marijuana.

WEEKEND HABIT. Someone who uses drugs on a casual, occasional basis.

WHACK. Same as **WACK.**

WHEAT. Slang for **MARIJUANA.**

WHITE LADY. Slang for **COCAINE.**

WHITE LIGHT. A vision of a blinding bright light, sometimes seen in the hallucinations that follow taking a drug such as STP.

WHITES. Slang for **AMPHETAMINES.**

WHITE STUFF. Slang for **HEROIN,** but also sometimes used to mean cocaine or morphine.

WHITE TORNADO. Slang for **COCAINE FREEBASE.**

WHIZ BANG. A mixture of either cocaine and heroin or cocaine and morphine.

WIG. The mind.

WILD GERONIMO. A drink consisting of a barbiturate dissolved in alcohol.

WINDOW PANE. LSD on a thin pane of gelatin, plastic, or cellophane.

WINGDING. Imitating someone who is suffering the pains of withdrawal in the hope of getting a doctor to prescribe narcotics.

WINOS. Vagrants or bums who keep themselves intoxicated on cheap wine. Winos usually panhandle for money in the streets, eat in soup kitchens, and sleep in cheap, run-down hotels called flop houses.

WIPED OUT. Highly intoxicated from drug use.

WIRED. Addicted to heroin.

WITHDRAWAL SYMPTOMS. A cluster of reactions and behavior patterns that follow a sudden stop in the use of a drug on which the person has become physically dependent. The actual symptoms vary considerably from person to person depending on the severity of the habit and the particular drug involved. In general, the withdrawal symptoms for narcotics may include anxiety, restlessness, aches, insomnia, perspiration, hot flashes, nausea, diarrhea, faster breathing, cramps, and loss of body weight. For barbiturates, the symptoms may include tremor, weakness, dizziness, visual distortion, weight loss, nausea, lowered blood pressure, anxiety, convulsions, seizures, and psychotic reactions. For alcohol, the symptoms may include tremors, sweating, nausea, rapid heartbeat, rise in temperature, convulsions, and delirium tremens.

WORKS. Equipment for injecting drugs.

X, X-T-C. Two other names for the drug called Ecstasy.

Y

YELLOW JACKETS. Slang for **NEMBUTAL**; the name comes from the color of the capsule.

YELLOWS. Slang for **NEMBUTAL**.

YEN. Originally a craving for opium, from the Chinese yen-yen, "opium habit." Now, any craving or desire.

YEN HOK. The long, thin needle on which opium is cooked before being smoked.

YENNING. Experiencing the symptoms of withdrawal from narcotics.

YEN POK. A small pellet of opium that has been cooked and is ready for smoking.

YERBA. Slang for **MARIJUANA.** The word comes from the Spanish, *hierba,* meaning "weed."

Z

ZIG-ZAG. A brand of paper used for rolling marijuana cigarettes.

ZOMBIE BUZZ. A very potent PCP that is brown in color.

ZOMBIE WEED. Marijuana with added PCP.

ZONKED. So intoxicated by a drug that one is completely unable to function.

FOR FURTHER INFORMATION

Al-Anon
One Park Avenue
New York, NY 10016

Alateen
One Park Avenue
New York, NY 10016

Alcoholics Anonymous (AA)
P. O. Box 459
Grand Central Station
New York, NY 10017

Alcoholism Center for Women
1147 S. Alvarado Street
Los Angeles, CA 90006

American Council for Drug Education
5820 Hubbard Drive
Rockville, MD 20852

American Council on Marijuana and Other Psychoactive Drugs (ACM)
6193 Executive Blvd.
Rockville, MD 20852

Cocaine Helpline
1-800-662-HELP

Do-It-Now Foundation
P. O. Box 5115
Phoenix, AZ 85010

Drug Enforcement Administration (DEA)
Office of Public Affairs
1405 I Street, N.W.
Washington, DC 20012

Narcotics Anonymous (NA)
World Service Office
P. O. Box 622
Sun Valley, CA 91352

Narcotics Education and Rehabilitation Foundation
P. O. Box 4330
Washington, DC 20012

Narcotics Education, Inc.
Box 4390
6830 Laurel Street, N.W.
Washington, DC 20012

National Association of State Alcohol and Drug Abuse Directors
918 F Street, N.W.
Suite 400
Washington, DC 20004

National Clearinghouse for Alcohol Information
Box 2345
Rockville, MD 20857

National Clearinghouse for
Drug Abuse Information
P. O. Box 416
Kensington, MD 20795

National Clearinghouse for
Smoking and Health
5600 Fishers Lane
Rockville, MD 20857

National Cocaine Hotline
1-800-COCAINE

National Council on Alcoholism
733 Third Avenue
New York, NY 10017

National Council on Drug
Abuse
571 West Jackson Avenue
Chicago, IL 60606

National Drug Abuse Center
5530 Wisconsin Avenue, N.W.
Suite 1600
Washington, DC 20015

National Institute on Alcohol
Abuse and Alcoholism
5600 Fishers Lane
Rockville, MD 20857

National Institute on Drug
Abuse
5600 Fishers Lane
Rockville, MD 20857

National Self-Help
Clearinghouse
33 West 42nd Street
New York, NY 10036

Parent Resource Institute on
Drug Education
100 Edgewood Avenue
Suite 1002
Atlanta, GA 30303

Parents for Drug Free Youth
8730 Georgia Avenue, N.W.
Suite 200
Silver Spring, MD 20910
Hotline: 1-800-554-KIDS

Prevention Materials Institute
Pacific Institute for Research and
Evaluation
P. O. Box 152
Lafayette, CA 94549

REFERENCES

Abel, Ernest L. *A Dictionary of Drug Abuse Terms and Terminology.* Westport, CT: Greenwood Press, 1984.

Aldrich, Dr. Michael, Richard Ashley and Michael Horowitz. *High Times Encyclopedia of Recreational Drugs.* New York: Stonehill Publishing Co., 1978.

Berger, Gilda. *Addiction.* New York: Franklin Watts, 1982.

───── *Crack.* New York: Franklin Watts, 1987.

Lingeman, Richard R. *Drugs from A to Z.* (Second Edition.) New York: McGraw-Hill, 1974.

Nelson, Jack E., Helen Wallenstein Pearson, Mollie Sayers and Thomas J. Glynn, eds. *Guide to Drug Abuse Research Terminology.* Rockville, MD: National Institute on Drug Abuse, 1982.

O'Hyde, Margaret *Mind Drugs.* (Fifth Edition.) New York: Dodd, Mead, 1986.

O'Brien, Robert and Sidney Cohen. *The Encyclopedia of Drug Abuse.* New York: Facts on File, 1984.